·PEMBRC

Map labels

CARDIGAN

Cardigan

Cenarth

Newcastle Emlyn

CARMARTHEN

St Clears

Whitland

Laugharne

Pendine

Teifi

Taf

A487 · B4333 · B4570 · A484 · B4332 · A478 · B4299 · B4298 · A40 · B4314 · A477 · A4066

Carmarthen Bay

Right: *The picturesque harbour at Tenby is extremely popular with visitors.*

Pembrokeshire is most famously known for the wild beauty of its coast, and rightly so. That is only the icing on the cake, however; there are many other rich ingredients. In this small peninsula, which is to Wales what Cornwall is to England, there exists a wealth of monuments bequeathed by our forebears – the remains of forts and settlements of Bronze Age people and Iron Age Celts; St Davids, the cradle of early Christianity in Wales; and the fine castles of the Normans who settled in the south of the county, indirectly causing it later to become an outpost of the English language. Other incomers – Vikings, Danes, Irish and Flemish among them – contributed to the county's history and influenced its culture. Behind bastions of cliffs lies a hinterland of fertile farmland, peaceful villages, tree-lined lanes and estuarine waters offering a mix of scenery much like parts of Devon and Cornwall but less crowded; and as they have Dartmoor and Exmoor, so Pembrokeshire has its own smaller wilderness of the Preseli Hills. Today a network of good roads speeds the visitor around the county without impinging on its tranquillity and beauty.

BEFORE 1066

Main picture: *Pentre Ifan, one of the best-preserved ancient burial chambers in Pembrokeshire, has a 16-ton capstone balanced on three uprights.*

Above: The cromlech of Carreg Sampson overlooks the Irish Sea near Abercastle.

The early Stone Age people who inhabited Pembrokeshire left little other than the detritus of their cave homes — tools of stone and antler and bones of the animals they hunted for food. The Neolithic and later Stone Age people, who arrived about 5,000 years ago, have left us many monuments of their culture, the most dominant being their chambered tombs or cromlechs — massive capstones precariously balanced on three or more stone pillars. These were the entrances to mausoleums, or barrows, in which the dead were deposited. Both the entrances and barrows were originally covered with earth which has long since eroded, leaving only the stark entrance stones still standing.

There are 15 cromlechs in the county, the most impressive being at Pentre Ifan, near Nevern. Three others well worth visiting are King's Quoit on the coast at Manorbier, Carreg Coetan in Newport, and Carreg Sampson. It was about 4,000 years ago that the 'blue' stones were transported from the Preseli Hills to Stonehenge.

Far more prolific, but less dramatic, are the standing stones, or menhirs, mostly dating from the Bronze Age, of which no fewer than 70 can be seen. They come singly, in pairs, and in alignments, but only Gors Fawr in the Preseli Hills forms a circle. The reason for these stones is a puzzle. They may have been burial markers, or phallic cult objects, or waymarks along ancient tracks; only a few generations ago many of them were painted white for that purpose. Today the only white menhir is by Rhodiad-y-Brenin farm near St Davids, where it marks the way to a guest house.

The Celtic Druids appropriated many Stone Age monuments for their own ceremonies, and in the Dark Ages and early Christian times many stones acquired mystical significance, not least by association with King Arthur. The later inscribing of Latin, Ogham and even early Welsh on some has further muddled their provenance. Of greater certainty and beauty are the Christian decorated wheel-head crosses such as those at Nevern, Carew and Penally, all examples of the superb standard of craftsmanship the ecclesiastical stone-masons had achieved by the 10th and 11th centuries. Almost as numerous as

standing stones, but usually only visible to hillwalkers, are the hillforts of the Iron Age Celts who brought their advanced iron technology to Wales in about 500BC, and their culture remained intact here until after the Roman period; the Romans left no monuments. The Celtic aristocracy lived in forts, while the peasants dwelt in scattered huts in the surrounding countryside. On many hills only a few bumps and stones can be discerned now. On the best sites, sections of defensive walls and round stone houses are well defined. The most interesting is Castell Henllys, near Nevern, which is being painstakingly excavated. Bigger and higher (1,140ft/347m), but unex-cavated, is Carningli (Hill of the Angels), which dominates the western horizon from Castell Henllys, and similar are Foel Drygarn in the Preseli Hills and Garn Fawr on the coast near Fishguard.

Below: The west face of the 6th-century Celtic wheel-head cross at Carew, which has an added 11th-century inscription.

Above: At Castell Henllys, some of the above-ground buildings, such as round huts, granaries and other outbuildings, are being reconstructed and furnished as they would have been during the Iron Age.

THE NORMANS

Below right: The Normans established a frontier — the Landsker Line — which divided the south of Pembrokeshire from the Welsh-speaking north. The line was defended by a string of castles, including Llawhaden, shown here.

Below: Statue of Llywelyn ab Iorwerth at Conwy, Gwynedd.

In Britain during the Dark Ages, following the departure of the Romans, the indigenous Britons (ancestors of the modern Welsh) were relentlessly driven westwards by Anglo-Saxon and Danish invaders. By the start of the 7th century, the power of the Britons had been broken everywhere, except within an area little larger than modern Wales where they retained their Celtic independence, governed by a number of petty princes, or 'kings'. From the time of King Offa of Mercia, modern Wales began to take shape. He extended his frontier west to include Shrewsbury, and by 784AD had dug a defensive dyke between Chester and Chepstow as a 'trip wire' against Welsh invaders. A succession of English kings waged inconclusive wars against parts of Wales until Harold was more successful, an outcome which led to the supremacy, in theory at least, of the English monarch over the Welsh princes.

Consequently, in 1066 William the Conqueror became overlord of Wales. He appointed three of his earls — Chester, Shrewsbury and Hereford — as Marcher Lords to guard his English frontier. There were constant border fights, and after the death of Rhys ap Tewdwr, the paramount prince of south Wales, the Normans were quick to invade his former territory. Their forces were led by Montgomery of Shrewsbury, who established his stronghold on a rocky eminence at the mouth of the Pembroke river. The site of his original wooden castle was to become in time one of the greatest castles in the country.

The Normans were of French origin and the toughest fighters in Europe. They were also great builders of castles — they erected 50 in Pembrokeshire. Being land-hungry, their first aim was to colonize the fertile coastal lands in the south of the country and deny them to the Welsh in the north. They achieved this by means of a chain of castles, among them Roch, Haverfordwest, Wiston, Llawhaden and, further north, Newport, Fishguard and Cardigan, while a string along the coast secured their supplies from the sea.

William II adopted the plan of granting conquered land to his barons wherever they successfully attacked the Welsh. Henry I settled Flemish immigrants, skilled in commerce and the woollen industry, in the region between Haverfordwest and Narberth 'for the purpose of civilizing the Welsh'. Stephen was a weak leader who allowed the barons in Pembroke to increase their feudal power; this served to cause further hostility among the Welsh.

Early in the 13th century, there was a revival of Welsh power when Llywelyn ab Iorwerth sided with the barons

Above: Statues of Edward I and Queen Eleanor at Lincoln Cathedral.

against King John, and threw out the English garrisons at Carmarthen and Cardigan on the Pembrokeshire borders. His grandson, Llywelyn ap Gruffudd, also sided with the barons against Henry III and was acknowledged as Prince of Wales with the right of receiving homage from the Welsh nobles. He refused to pay homage to Edward I as overlord of Wales, and this led to Edward's expeditions into the country and the final conquest of the Principality in 1284. English law and administration were established, and the country was divided into counties, one of which was Pembrokeshire.

Above left: Roch Castle.

Above: William the Conqueror at his coronation in Westminster Abbey on Christmas Day 1066, from Wavrin's Chroniques d'Angleterre, written and illuminated in Flanders for Edward IV of England.

PEMBROKE AND ITS GREAT CASTLE

Main picture: In its time, Pembroke Castle was the greatest Norman fortress in Wales.

Below: Aerial view of the castle, showing the outer and inner walls, gatehouse and keep.

The history of Pembroke began in 1093, when Roger de Montgomery, Earl of Shrewsbury, leading a Norman invasion of south-west Wales, established his timber castle on top of a limestone promontory overlooking the waters of Milford Haven. From that near-impregnable position, with vertical cliffs and the river defending three sides, Montgomery and his successors dominated the Anglo-Norman occupation of most of Pembrokeshire. By the time of Henry I (1100–1135), the castle had a town with a charter, market, mint and a port which ensured supplies from the sea in times of trouble, and exported coal, wool, lime and other products to the profit of the townsfolk.

The stone castle, the substantial ruins of which can be seen today, was first built by another Marcher Lord, William Marshall, and his five sons, between 1189 and 1245. The huge keep dominates the curtain walls, which were later extended to encompass the town. The landward length of the outer walls was reinforced by a barbican and five great towers. An inner wall and gatehouse provided a second defence for the inner ward which overlooks the steepest section of cliffs.

The course of British history has twice been irreversibly changed by men who were born in Pembroke Castle. In 1169 Richard de Clare, the second Earl of Pembroke, better known as Strongbow, sailed out of Milford Haven for Ireland with an army of mounted knights-in-mail, foot-soldiers, archers ('the flower of the

youth of Wales') with their deadly bows, and a contingent of Flemish settlers. Strongbow was acting in support of Dermot, the deposed High King of Leinster, who had declared 'gold and silver I shall give them, a very ample pay; whoever may wish for soil or sod, richly shall I endow them', a promise that no Norman lord could resist. He also threw in the hand of his daughter Eva. Strongbow defeated an Irish-Viking army at Wexford, won Dermot's daughter, marched to Dublin which he captured, and in due course became High King of Leinster.

On 28 January 1457, Henry Tudor was born in Pembroke Castle to Margaret Beaufort, the 15-year-old widow of the Lancastrian Earl of Richmond. At the age of 26, Henry was exiled to Brittany after the collapse of the Lancastrian cause in the Wars of the Roses. He swore to return, kill the usurper Richard III and marry Elizabeth of York, so uniting the red and white roses for the peace of the realm. Two years later he sailed into Mill Bay by St Ann's Head and, with a scratch force of Bretons and local Welshmen, he began an extraordinary two-week march to Bosworth Field, raising an army of supporters on the way. There Richard III famously lost his horse and his crown, which Henry Tudor placed on his own head. Thus began the Tudor dynasty which set the red dragon of Wales alongside the lion of England on the royal coat-of-arms.

Above: *Portrait of Henry Tudor, who was born in Pembroke Castle, in the Henry VII tower.*

Below: *The 80ft (24m) high, drum-shaped Norman keep was the mightiest in Europe.*

ST DAVID AND HIS CATHEDRAL

The cathedral of St Davids derives its name from the tutelary saint of Wales and all Welshmen. He was born of mixed British and Irish princely lines in the early 6th century. After a long period of studying literature and divinity, he established his religious house near to his birthplace, where the cathedral now stands. His followers had to observe a law of silence, and their time was divided between prayer and hard manual labour. They wore animal skins, and subsisted on a basic diet of salted bread, roots, herbs and watered milk. Despite this harsh regime, both the place and its founder rapidly gained in repute.

He was offered the Archbishopric of Caerleon, which he accepted on condition that he could move the see to the site of his own religious house. He died on 1 March (now St David's Day) in about 589. In 1120 he was canonized by Pope Calixtus II, who decreed that two pilgrimages to his shrine equated with one to Rome. Twenty Welsh bishops succeeded David before the Norman clergy took control of the church in Wales in 1115 and St Davids came under the auspices of Canterbury. No trace has been found of the original church of thatch-and-daub, but it was important enough to be raided ten times by the Vikings and visited by William the Conqueror.

The present Norman cathedral, built in a hollow to hide it from marauders, was started by a Florentine monk, Peter de Leia, some time before 1178. It was 300 years in the building, during which time the tower fell down and it suffered damage from an earthquake. It has been much restored and added to over the centuries, not least by Sir George Gilbert Scott (1811–98). De Leia's nave is in the late-Norman style, with clustered pillars supporting round arches with another arcade of arches above them. Its muted sandstone contrasts with the wooden ceiling, and the fan vault above Holy Trinity Chapel is reminiscent of that in Henry VII's chapel in Westminster Abbey. An iron-bound oak casket in a jewelled reliquary is believed to contain the bones of St David and his

Below: The nave of St Davids Cathedral has a richly decorated wooden ceiling.

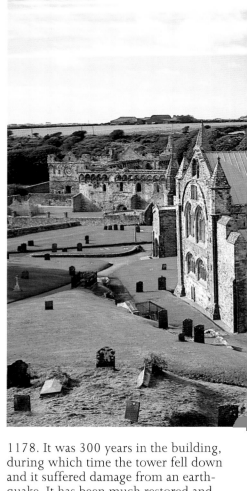

Below: The holy well of St Non, St David's mother, stands near her chapel on the cliffs to the south of the cathedral.

Inset left: The well-preserved wheel window in the ruins of the Bishop's Palace.

Left: From the city, the cathedral is first glimpsed by visitors only at the last moment as they descend a steep lane leading to a gatehouse in the 13th-century walls.

Below: The architectural style of this chapel, built in 1934 near to the original St Non's Chapel, now ruined, is based on that of similar early buildings.

confessor, St Justinian. In 1500, a number of humorous scenes were carved on the misericords in the choir stalls.

South of the cathedral are the roofless ruins of the Bishop's Palace, an exuberant work founded in 1340 by Bishop Henry de Gower, with a ceremonial hall 88ft (27m) long and lit by a great wheel window. It is an impressive ruin embellished with arcaded parapets. One mile (1.6km) away, looking out over the sea at St Non's Bay, is the lonely little ruin of St Non's Chapel and holy well; St Non was St David's mother, and the chapel is presumed to mark his birthplace.

THE COAST

Far right: The 'Green Bridge of Wales', looking towards St Govan's Head.

Above: St Ann's Head makes a superb viewpoint from which to watch ships plying to and from Milford Haven as well as yachts using the marinas of Milford Haven and Neyland, and the inland moorings up the Daugleddau.

The coastline of Pembrokeshire – sculpted by Atlantic gales yet cosseted by the warm currents of the Gulf Stream – is surely what most visitors come to admire and remember best. With its majestic cliffs, offshore islands, fjords, rocky coves, estuaries, incomparable sands and rich wildlife, it is without rival in Europe.

Nowhere is the sea or its inland tidal reaches further away than 8 miles (13km), and a web of small lanes leads to miniature harbours squeezed between vertical rocks, and to beaches with miles of firm golden sand and safe swimming. Ample car parks cater for families, sea anglers, divers, windsurfers, water-skiers and people with small boats.

Walkers can follow the 186-mile (300km) Coastal Path which encircles the National Park. Much of the path keeps close to the edge of vertiginous

ST GOVAN'S CHAPEL

From the village of Bosherston a lane leads to a clifftop car park above St Govan's little 13th-century oratory, wedged into a cleft and reached by 53 precipitous stone steps. It is a fine early Christian monument, plain and unadorned apart from a stone altar, bench and empty bellcote, and was built around the original 5th-century cell of the saint. His holy well, now dry, can be found nearby amid the boulders. A short walk to the west is the Huntsman's Leap – the huntsman is said to have died of shock when he looked back to see the chasm he had crossed.

10 miles (16km) to the west, sheer limestone cliffs rise 150ft (45m) out of the sea and are topped by a perfectly flat plateau, presenting a seemingly impregnable defence against the fury of the Atlantic. They have withstood the sea for 150,000 years, but the great boulders at their feet are the sea's trophies from its relentless war against the land. More subtly, in places the waves have eaten into the softer rock, carving out coves and caves, and cutting tunnels and arches through promontories.

Just below St Ann's Head is the tiny, east-facing cove of Mill Bay where, on 7 August 1485, Henry Tudor landed on his way to Bosworth Field. Access to the bays on the west flank of St Ann's is difficult, and strong undertows should deter bathers. In contrast, Dale on the east side is a sheltered swimming beach and yacht anchorage beside pink-washed cottages backed by wooded hills. It is reminiscent of a picture-postcard Cornish village, which is perhaps appropriate as this is a very English part of the Little England of Pembrokeshire where names like Marloes, St Bride's, Philbeach Farm and Kensington House will strike a chord with those familiar with parts of south-west London.

Above: The wide, sweeping bays of Pembrokeshire make a perfect setting for wind-surfing enthusiasts, as well as for families enjoying more leisurely seaside pursuits.

Below: The Pembrokeshire Coastal Path takes in some of the most stunning and varied scenery in the British Isles, from level sandy beaches to precip-itous cliffs crowned by a carpet of flowers. In some places the walk can be challenging.

cliffs and ragged headlands with sea on three sides. To complete its length would involve 35,000ft (10,670m) of ascent and descent, with some difficult stretches best suited to fine weather and fit walkers; but the route also takes in gentle shorelines and beaches that offer the tactile pleasure of walking barefoot across miles of sand.

Around St Govan's Head – the most southerly point of Wales – and for

Main picture: White-sands Bay boasts a beautiful stretch of sandy beach, from where St Patrick is said to have set sail for Ireland.

The isolated crescent of Marloes Sands has an alien planet appearance with its fang-shaped outcrop of rocks round which the hurrying tide hisses and froths. Under a lowering sky or in the red glow of sunset, the scene is particularly photogenic. The Sands are backed by an amphitheatre of red and yellow cliffs, 400 million years old, which are of great interest to geologists, as are the Three Chimneys, a row of once-horizontal rock layers which were caused to stand up on end by an ancient upheaval. From the end of the Sands the island of Gateholm and its Iron Age fort are accessible at low tide.

Another London connection is Marloes Mere, where in Victorian days the locals harvested leeches for doctors in Harley Street. The edible seaweed found on Marloes Sands and Mussel-wick Sands to the north of the village is harvested to make laver bread.

At the end of every lane or farm road leading to the seashore can be found the remains of lime kilns. Raw limestone brought by sea was burned in the kilns to make lime for the farmland. Once every little harbour had its fleet of family fishing boats, and the

A SECRET WATER

In the heart of Pembrokeshire there lies a little-known sanctuary called the Daugleddau, a water-way formed by four tidal rivers – the Eastern and Western Cleddau, the Cress-well and the Carew. They once formed a busy commercial highway taking the

products of quarries, collieries, mills, farms and boatyards down to the Milford estuary and out to sea. The coming of the railways changed all that, and today the Daugleddau is left in peace to the birds and the sailors whose boats lie in mud berths. To explore the area, you must go by boat or walk – there are 90 miles (145km) of interconnecting routes of the Daugleddau Trail. Sites of interest on the Trail are Blackpool Mill, and the castles of Carew, Picton and Benton.

quays were kept busy exporting coal, iron ore and the products of wool and corn mills, of which two – at Carew and Blackpool – have been renovated for the interest of visitors. Porthgain was built to export bricks and road stone, and the nearby Blue Lagoon at Abereiddy, a local beauty spot on the west coast, is in fact a worked-out slate quarry flooded and kept refreshed by each high tide. It is also a site of international importance with a rare marine ecosystem sheltering squirts, bristle worms, sponges and its famous tuning-fork rocks, or trapto-lites, which oscillate when knocked. The broken ruins of the quarry build-ings and tramway have long since merged into the ragged slate on which they stood.

Below: Marloes Sands, backed by spectacular rocky cliffs, is a good surfing beach and safe for swimming.

Below: The best exam-ple of lime kilns is this pair at Porth Clais, near St Davids, restored by the National Trust.

ISLANDS

Main picture: Skomer, off the Marloes Peninsula, run by Dyfed Wildlife Trust, is the most accessible island for observing wildlife; boats make the short crossing regularly.

The Pembrokeshire coast boasts 16 offshore islands. An exciting day can be spent seeing all of them from a motor vessel run by Thousand Island Expeditions. All are now uninhabited (except by the wardens in the summer), apart from Caldey, where the tourist attraction is the monastery. Skomer, Skokholm, Ramsey and Grassholm are, first and foremost, nature reserves where puffins, razorbills, guillemots, kittiwakes, gannets and other seabirds can breed in peace, yet be seen at close quarters from a boat.

With a nesting population of some quarter of a million birds, Skomer was the first Marine Nature Reserve in Wales. The cliff ledges are home to 32,000 breeding pairs of gannets. On the clifftops the puffins, fussing around their burrows, share their territory with 100,000 pairs of manx shearwaters, which travel far out to sea to feed. Other possible sightings are choughs, falcons and short-eared owls, as well as the unique Skomer vole. In late spring and early summer, the island is carpeted with wild flowers, which can be found among the remains of Iron Age stone hut circles. Its sheer cliffs plunge deep into the sea with its coloured seaweeds, corals, iridescent anemones, sponges and sea squirts.

The neighbouring island of Skokholm (both are run by Dyfed

CALDEY ISLAND MONASTERY

The Cistercian monks of Caldey Island are best known for the perfume they produce and the strict rule of silence they observe, but they also keep cattle. Boats run out of Tenby to Caldey Island from the Spring Holiday to late September four times an hour. Visitors may attend mass in the Abbots Chapel each afternoon at 2.30, but tours of the monastery are available only to men. There is a nature reserve noted for its cormorants on adjoining St Margaret's Isle which can be viewed from the boat to and from Caldey, but no one is allowed ashore.

Below left: On the grassy clifftops, puffins emerge from their burrows to feed on sand eels.

Bottom left: Grey seals and their pups can be seen in large numbers on Grassholm Island during the autumn months.

Wildlife Trust) was Britain's first bird observatory. From April to September migrants such as warblers, flycatchers and waders add to the resident birdlife, joined at night by thousands of manx shearwaters and storm petrels. The Trust provides board and lodging for up to 15 visitors a week, but there is no electricity so evenings are spent around a tilley lamp; everyone has to share the domestic chores.

Grassholm, with the second largest gannetry in the northern hemisphere, is 10 miles (16km) offshore; dolphins may be seen in the surrounding water.

Round trips start in May, but landing is not allowed until mid-June and boats do not go every day. Ramsey Island, reached by boat from St Justinian's near St Davids, is an RSPB reserve comparable to, but smaller than, Skomer, with visitors limited to 40 a day. Autumn sees the largest concentration of Atlantic grey seals in southern Britain when they come ashore to give birth to their white pups.

Below: Skomer's floral carpet, which includes sea pinks or thrift, is a delight to behold in spring and summer.

Useful telephone numbers
Thousand Island Expeditions: 01437 721686
Dyfed Wildlife Trust: 01437 765462
Dale Sailing Co. (boats to islands): 01646 601636

THE PRESELI HILLS

Above: Welsh mountain ponies still roam wild through the undulating Preseli moorland.

Below: The cairns and hillfort of Foel Drygarn create a dramatic and mysterious focal point within the Pembrokeshire Coast National Park.

In the wilderness of the Preseli Hills you can find peace away from the throng, and walk below broad skies over moorland coloured with purple heather and yellow gorse, among rounded hills with distant vistas. The Hills are dotted with cairns and standing stones, but boast only one stone circle – Gors Fawr near Mynachlogddu which is located to the west of the Narberth–Cardigan road.

For a strong sense of history, take the minor road north out of Mynachlogddu to Foel Drygarn, to see the 220 Iron Age hut circles, two stone walls and three cairns on its 1,190ft (363m) summit. From there join a section of the Bronze Age Track, along which 3,000 years ago copper and gold were brought from the mountains of Wicklow to the plains of Wessex. It is well marked on the OS Landranger map, a red dotted line passing the foot of Foel Drygarn and threading west through the whirling contour lines. It offers one of the best walks in the county.

After skirting the top edge of a conifer plantation, the Track passes a group of crags

along a ridge named Carn Menyn. It was from there, some 4,000 years ago, that the 80 'blue' stones were transported – no one knows exactly how – 240 miles (386km) to Salisbury Plain to form the inner circle of Stonehenge. There is a theory that they were carried by glacier during the Ice Age, but it is more probable that they were moved on wooden rollers to the Eastern Cleddau and from there rafted via Milford Haven, the Bristol Channel and several rivers, eventually to be hauled up to Stonehenge. It is wonderful to stand among those crags and consider how such a feat could have been achieved.

The Track climbs west, passing several cairns, before reaching the foot of Foel Cwmcerwyn, at 1,760ft (536m) the highest point of the Preseli Hills. It has four Bronze Age burial cairns on its summit, and on its eastern flank a steep-sided Ice Age moraine. From that high point, return to the Track, which continues along the north edge of

Pantmaenog Forest to meet the B4329, after which it curls round Cerrig Lladron from whose 1,535ft (468m) summit there is a spectacular view of the steep, wooded Gwaun Valley winding its way to Lower Fishguard. There are five old churches in the valley and an alignment of eight standing stones. Designated a Site of Special Scientific Interest, it is well worth visiting. While the Bronze Age Track goes on to the west coast at Whitesands Bay, from where St Patrick set sail for Ireland, the walker can turn south down the B4329 to the crossroads at New Inn, and take some refreshment in the pub there.

While in the Hills, beware of bogland and the low cloud or thick mist which can cover the hilltops, even in summer. Stout footwear is needed, and a compass and map should be carried even when following marked ways, as it is easy to get lost.

Left: The 16 small stones of Gors Fawr, none higher than 3ft (1m), form a circle 70ft (21m) across; nearby are two man-sized standing stones.

Left: Carn Menyn, the source of the Stonehenge 'blue' stones.

◆ LAUGHARNE

The Castle at Laugharne, just over the border into Carmarthenshire, overlooks the Taf estuary near the Boat House where Dylan Thomas lived during the last four years of his life. Here in his 'writing shed' he wrote *Under Milk Wood*. He lived in two other homes in the town before moving into the Boat House in 1949. The poet is remembered by the locals of Brown's Hotel, where he spent much time drinking with friends.

◆ LOWER FISHGUARD

The most notable site in this charming town is the Royal Oak, where the last invasion of Britain in 1797 was formally ended by the signing of a surrender in the bar. The fishermen's cottages round the old harbour at the mouth of the Gwaun river were the setting for the film of *Under Milk Wood*. During the American War of Independence, the privateer Paul Jones fired two broadsides into the town to force the payment of a 500 guineas ransom. Gwaun valley is a peaceful haven where New Year's Day is still observed on 13 January, as it was before the Julian calendar. Along the river can be found inscribed stones dating from the 7th century, and a string of small, bellcoted churches.

Above right: The Boat House, Laugharne.

Right: The old harbour, Lower Fishguard.

✦ NARBERTH AND THE LANDSKER

The Normans established a frontier – the Landsker Line – which divided the Anglo-Norman-speaking south of Pembrokeshire from the Welsh-speaking north. The line was defended by a string of castles, including Roch, Llawhaden, Haverfordwest, Wiston, Narberth and Amroth. The area along that frontier is now called the Landsker Borderlands, a ribbon of rural peace with a web of waymarked trails. Narberth is the 'capital', and within its Landsker Visitor Centre the folk tales of the *Mabinogion* are illustrated on large panels and retold by the resident storyteller, just as they would have been before being committed to paper in the 11th century.

✦ NEVERN

This riverside village is hidden in a wooded valley not far from the busy Newport-Cardigan road. It has a wealth of antiquities, and a mystery too – by the churchyard gate there is an ancient yew which 'bleeds' blood-red sap. The church, of Norman origins with a 12th-century tower but largely 15th-century perpendicular, is dedicated to the Irish St Brynach. It has a 15th-century Celtic Ogham- and Latin-inscribed stone on a window sill, and a late 10th-century or early 11th-century wheel-head cross, 13ft (4m) high and elaborately carved. On the Frongoch road is the Pilgrim's Cross, a rock incised with a cross, below which is a hollow where pilgrims to St David's are said to have knelt. On the edge of a gorge above the Caman river, there are remains of a motte and bailey, which replaced the stronghold of a Welsh chieftain. Among some fine houses in the parish are Trewern, a Jacobean mansion, and Llwyngwair Manor, now a hotel.

Below left: A scene from one of the tales of the Mabinogion, *Landsker Visitor Centre.*

Below right: Celtic cross outside the church at Nevern.

Bottom: St Brynach's Church, Nevern.

Above: Some salmon fishermen still use coracles on the river Teifi.

Right: With a sunny harbour filled with colourful boats and surrounded by Georgian and Regency houses, Tenby is the most attractive town on the coast.

✦ RIVER TEIFI AND CORACLES

The Teifi, famous for its salmon and sea trout, is one of the finest rivers in Wales. Poppit Sands, at its mouth, is the most northerly beach within the Pembrokeshire Coast National Park and the start of the Coastal Path. On the shore upstream from Cardigan stand the ruins of Cilgerran Castle, built around 1108; over the following 100 years or so it was won and lost several times between the Normans and Welsh. The remains seen today are those of a later building founded in 1223 and ruined at the end of the 14th century. In medieval times, Cilgerran was an inland port reached by seagoing ships. Coracles – shallow one-man craft of pitch-soaked calico stretched over wickerwork frames – have been used for centuries by salmon fishermen. At the National Coracle Centre in Cenarth in Carmarthenshire there is a collection of coracles from all over the world.

✦ SAUNDERSFOOT AND TENBY

Saundersfoot first appeared on the map in 1829 when a harbour was built for the export of anthracite from minings in the Begelly, Kilgetty and Stepaside areas. The last mine was closed in 1939, and after the war the port was developed as one of the finest yacht harbours in Wales. There are sheltered sands north and south of the town. Tenby dates back to the 14th century when a town grew up around a 12th-century castle. Little remains of that, but the town walls are among the most complete in the country. The National Trust have renovated and furnished the 15th-century Merchant's House near the harbour. Tenby also boasts four pleasant sandy beaches.

Right: Tenby Castle.

Back cover: Tenby harbour.

Steam on the Great E
Norfolk and Suffolk

Compiled by Alan C Butcher

The
· Transport ·
Treasury

© Images and design: The Transport Treasury 2021. Text Alan C Butcher.

ISBN 978-1-913251-24-6

First published in 2021 by Transport Treasury Publishing Ltd., 16 Highworth Close, High Wycombe, HP13 7PJ

www.ttpublishing.co.uk

Printed in the UK by Henry Ling Limited at the Dorset Press, Dorchester. DT1 1HD

Front Cover: For many decades East Anglia was a holiday destination of choice, before air travel increased the options available, with many Saturday only services running for a few weeks during the summer timetable. Not all services were operated over the main lines as it was often easier to make use of lighter used routes such as this Manchester-Clacton train seen approaching Welnetham on the single track Bury St Edmunds to Marks Tey route. This route avoided the need to reverse at Colchester as the junction there for Clacton faced south. No 61653 *Huddersfield Town* was a member of the LNER's 'B17/4' class dating from April 1936. Rebuilt to Class B17/6 specification in May 1954 it was withdrawn in January 1960; a year later this route would close to passenger traffic. *Dr Ian C Allen E2632*

Title page: A busy scene at King's Lynn as Class B12/3 No 61575 departs with a London Liverpool Street to Hunstanton express service passing Class J17 No 65533 as it does so. Following arrival at King's Lynn the express would have had to reverse to continue its run to 'sunny Hunny', with No 61575 providing the motive power for the final part of the journey. It was built by Beyer, Peacock, Manchester, in September 1928 and originally fitted with a small Belpaire boiler, later rebuilt with the round top version seen here. No 61575 was allocated to King's Lynn between April and November 1957, withdrawal occurring in April 1959. *Dr Ian C Allen E3298*

Opposite: Not all motive power on the former GER/LNER network was from its own design lineage, here double-headed London Midland & Scottish Railway Class 2MTs head an excursion train from Mildenhall to Skegness near Fordham Junction. However, both locomotives, Nos 46466 and 46477, were constructed at the former LNER's Darlington Works in June 1951; they would have taken the train as far as Ely where more powerful motive power would have taken over the 12-coach train for the journey northwards. *Dr Ian C Allen M645*

Rear Cover: The Waveney Valley line ran between Tivetshall and Beccles, opening in stages between 1855 and 1863. No 65469, seen here shunting at Bungay, was a member of the GER's 'Y14' class – reclassified by the LNER as 'J15' at the time of the Grouping in 1923. Constructed by the GER's Stratford Works in May 1912, it was in service for over 50 years as withdrawal came in August 1962. The 32A on the plate on the smokebox indicates that the locomotive was allocated to Norwich shed. *Dr Ian C Allen E1431*

Contents

Introduction

Following an Act of Parliament on 7th August 1862 the Great Eastern Railway (GER) was formed by the amalgamation of the Eastern Union, East Anglian, Norfolk, Eastern Counties, Newmarket and East Suffolk railways. Due to the poor financial status of the companies it inherited the GER was in a no better state, but managed to trade its way out of receivership. With a number of ports on the east coast the GER took the opportunity to develop ferry traffic to the continent using its own vessels – six ships were to become casualties during World War 1. The GER was to take over a large number of smaller independent companies before its network became part of the London & North Eastern Railway (LNER) at the grouping on 1st January 1923, and then British Railways (BR) – as part of the Eastern Region – on 1st January 1948.

As this is a photographic record, rather than a history, the reader is referred to the Bibliography and Further Reading list on page 112 for a more detailed record of the construction – and destruction – of the network.

The GER, followed by the LNER, was to help develop a number of holiday resorts along the north Norfolk and east coasts with direct services from London Liverpool Street during the holiday periods. Traffic from the industrial northwest was also developed with many services making use of the quieter secondary routes to avoid congestion of the main lines.

The LNER, and BR Eastern Region, were not shy in removing passenger services from stations and lines that were not contributing to income. The Denver-Stoke Ferry line lost its passenger services on 22nd September 1930; however general freight traffic on the line survived until 19th April 1965 with sugar beet traffic for several more years. The 1950s saw the closure to passenger traffic of several of the 'cross-country' routes, generally freight traffic would continue to the 1960s when much of the traffic was taken over by road transport.

Dr Richard Beeching's report on *The Reshaping of British Railways*, published in March 1963, only accelerated the government's desire to make the railways cover its costs. Although the rationalisation was by the governments of the day, the closures are generally referred to as being axed by Dr Beeching. The result was that many of the remaining lines had services reduced – only to result in their later closure due to ever decreasing number of passengers as private car ownership increased – as the remaining trains, and connections, were not timed to encourage people to use them. Even the holiday destinations of Hunstanton and Wells lost their remaining passenger services – the station site at 'sunny Hunny' is now the town's main car park. With today's increasing tourism, a 'park and ride' for Hunstanton would decrease road traffic congestion in the town and provide a commuter service into King's Lynn.

My previous title in this area using Dr Ian C. Allen's photographs – *First Generation Diesels in East Anglia* – concentrated on the counties of Suffolk and Norfolk working from south to north; to make a change this time we are running in a generally southwards direction to the Essex border – or 'Up' in railway terminology – as far as Marks Tey where the Stour Valley line connects to the GE main line.

General note: Unless otherwise stated all locomotives were constructed at the GER's Stratford Works; and to save a lot of repetition the North British Locomotive Co, Glasgow, (NBL) who built a number of the 'B1s' that were to see service on former GER metals. Following the Grouping, the LNER reclassified and renumbered the majority of the locomotives it inherited; so all classes should be regarded as the LNER designation unless otherwise stated. Some 150 individual locomotives are illustrated and details are generally given the first time it is mentioned.

Alan C Butcher.

Summer 2021.

Opposite top: We start our journey at Cromer High, the first station opened in the town and situated to the south on the outskirts on a steep escarpment some distance from the town itself. Built initially by the short-lived East Norfolk Railway, the station opened on 26th March 1877. It was (along with the line) incorporated into the GER, on 3rd June 1881, who had operated the services from the beginning. It served as the terminus of GER services from London and Norwich. Initially known as Cromer, it was renamed Cromer High on 27th September 1948, following nationalisation of the railways on 1st January that year. On 23rd July 1906 a connection was opened between the line to Cromer High and the Midland & Great Northern Joint Railway (M&GNJt) line between Melton Constable and Cromer Beach stations, allowing through trains from Norwich to run into the latter. As Cromer Beach was far more conveniently sited in the centre of the town, passenger numbers using Cromer High dropped substantially, although it remained in use as a freight depot. Passenger services ceased at Cromer High on 20th September 1954, with traffic diverted to Cromer Beach (renamed 'Cromer' in 1969). High remained open as a freight terminus until 7th March 1960; closed completely, the station was subsequently demolished. Cromer High station was situated a short distance away from the Cromer Tunnel, Norfolk's only standard gauge railway tunnel for passenger traffic to remain intact, connecting the Sheringham line to the Norfolk & Suffolk Joint Railway (N&SJt) route to Mundesley; all services ceased in April 1953. The crew of Class B17/6 No 61670 *City of London* acknowledge the photographer's presence. In 1937 No 61670, then numbered 2859, was one of two members of the class to receive 'A4'-like streamlined casings. Both locomotives had their streamline casing removed in 1951. *Dr Ian C Allen E3529*

Opposite bottom: Appearing in June 1911 as a GER Class G69 (LNER Class F6), No 67228 is seen standing by the turntable at Cromer High. The 65ft table replaced an earlier 45ft version, and looked out of place at the single road shed, although it enabled longer locomotives to be turned. One feature of the shed was the extended arm of the delivery pipe enabling locomotives on the turntable road to be watered, note the grounded van body being used as a store. *Dr Ian C Allen E923*

Cromer High to Norwich

Opposite top: Dr Allen would have taken this image out of the carriage window looking back as the train leaves Cromer High station. With the summer service requiring additional rolling stock when compared with the daily service, the carriages on the left were probably spending a week at the seaside pending their next journey. *Dr Ian C Allen E2742*

Opposite bottom: The station at Gunton opened on 29th July 1876, to serve a nonexistent village! The station is in the parish of Thorpe Market and closest to Lower Street. It was built primarily for the convenience of Lord Suffield, who lived at nearby Gunton Hall, a major investor in the original East Norfolk Railway which built the line from Norwich to Cromer. Originally the location of a passing loop, the northbound platform and station buildings are now privately owned. In September 1928 Class B12 No 8552 was photographed north of the station with an express bound for Cromer. The train ran non-stop between Liverpool Street and North Walsham, where the double track ended; it was difficult to ensure non-stop running over the single line to Cromer. No 8552 was built by Beardmore Ltd, Dalmure, Glasgow, in December 1920 as GER Class S69 No 1552. As well as the domestic market, William Beardmore & Co also built steam locomotives for operation overseas, mainly in India. *Dr Ian C Allen E612*

Above: Historically, North Walsham was served by two adjacent railway stations; the current station opening on 20th October 1874 served the GER line; next door was the former Midland & Great Northern Joint Railway's North Walsham Town station serving its lines to Melton Constable (either via Aylsham or via Mundesley-on-Sea and Sheringham) and Great Yarmouth (via Potter Heigham). North Walsham Town closed on 28th February 1959 with the 'Main' station renamed simply 'North Walsham'. Today the station is the site of the only passing loop on the route, which has been worked remotely from Norwich since the line was re-signalled in 2000. The station goods yard is the last operational freight location on the line, with regular bulk trainloads of gas concentrate (piped in from various offshore North Sea gas fields) from here to Harwich International. Aggregate traffic (in the form of spent railway ballast) has also been handled here in the past. The second member of Thompson's Class B1 to be constructed left Darlington Works in June 1943. No 61001 *Eland* is seen at North Walsham with a single open wagon and brake van in tow. Transferred from Neasden in September 1959, No 61001 was allocated to Norwich until December the same year, conveniently dating the period the photograph was taken. No 61001 survived in traffic until September 1963. *Dr Ian C Allen E1117*

Top: The station at Whitlingham was opened on 20th October 1874, being the last one on the line into Norwich – the junction with the Great Yarmouth and Lowestoft line being to the east of it. Closure to passenger traffic came on 19th September 1955 – well before the Beeching era. Freight traffic ended on 13th July 1964. Subsequently demolished, there is no sign of the station; however the footbridge is still in use for pedestrians over Whitlingham Lane level crossing. Just to the east of the station was Whitlingham junction where Class A5 4-6-2T No 69826 heads north over the junction, with a motley collection of carriages in tow, bound for Cromer. Built at Gorton Works in May 1923 to a John G. Robinson design for the Great Central Railway, No 69826 was allocated to Norwich between June 1952 and February 1956, surviving in traffic until June 1958.
Dr Ian C Allen E714

Bottom: In bound to Norwich from the Great Yarmouth/Lowestoft direction, 'F6' 2-4-2T No 67223 was one of 20 locomotives built to an S. D. Holden design for the GER at Stratford Works between April 1911 and January 1912. The GER was a prolific user of the 2-4-2T wheel arrangement with 242 built of which 235 were incorporated into the LNER at the Grouping. No 67223 was allocated to Lowestoft shed between October 1953 and December 1955 when it was withdrawn. *Dr Ian C Allen E2578*

A general view looking over Swing Bridge junction towards Wensum Yard just south of Norwich. The lines heading off to the left lead to Norwich Thorpe station with the lines to the right forming the avoiding line for services running direct to Cromer, Great Yarmouth and Lowestoft. Alongside the east-west running line are several stacks of track panels, either awaiting use or recycling as this area was used by the permanent way department. *Dr Ian C Allen MISC255*

These 0-4-0T locomotives were built by the Sentinel Steam Waggon Co in Shrewsbury. As LNER Class Y1, they were used for shunting duties at various locations. Built in December 1926 (as works No 6710) this example carried No 8401 when new and was renumbered 8131 under the LNER's 1946 scheme. It never carried its allocated BR one (68131) being transferred to departmental stock in August 1953 as No 39. It is seen shunting in Norwich Wensum Yard where it was in use at the Norwich Engineers Depot, surviving in service until April 1963. The Class 37 diesel in the background is heading towards Norwich Thorpe station, dating the image to the early 1960s. *Dr Ian C Allen E1587*

Top: The last junction before Norwich station is at Thorpe, here the Cromer, Yarmouth & Lowestoft lines are joined by the lines running in from the south. Running towards Norwich Thorpe station is No 67730, a member of Thompson's 'L1' class 2-6-4Ts designed in 1945 principally for working suburban services out of King's Cross and Marylebone. Only the first member of the class – No 9000 – entered service for the LNER, the remainder of the 100 strong class appeared after Nationalisation; No 67730 was the last member of the class built at Darlington in August 1948 – the balance being split between the NBL and Robert Stephenson & Hawthorn – and withdrawn in August 1962. *Dr Ian C Allen E1039*

Bottom: Almost at its destination No 90559 passes Norwich Thorpe junction on the approaches to the station. The goods shed and yard was alongside the current passenger station and occupied the site of the city's original one which was replaced in 1886. The Austerity 2-8-0s were constructed during World War 2 to help the war effort. The locomotive illustrated was built by Vulcan Foundry at its Newton-le-Willows works in September 1943 as No 77095. Following D-Day in June 1944 it was shipped across the Channel with its final depot being Antwerp Dam, Belgium. Following the cessation of hostilities the locomotives remaining in the UK, or repatriated, were loaned to the 'Big Four' companies; the LNER purchased 200 in 1946, whilst another 533 were on loan to BR at Nationalisation. No 77095 was renumbered by British Railways as No 90559 and was the only member of the class to be allocated to Norwich shed – from April 1959 to January 1960; it was withdrawn in December 1962 and recycled by the Central Wagon Co, Wigan. *Dr Ian C Allen BR244*

Norwich Locomotive Depot and Works were adjacent to the station on the south side of the line. Established in 1843 by the Y&NR, it was built and designed by William Marshall. By 1845 the shed was the centre of locomotive maintenance for the Norfolk Railway. The main shed consisted of four through roads, one of which dealt with everyday repairs and an adjacent site that dealt with more serious repairs. Like many GER engine sheds a lot of facilities were very basic. Ash (a waste product from the burning of coal) was dropped directly into an area known as the old yard where it was then shovelled into wagons. In the early days coal was unloaded from wagons onto a wooden stage and then loaded manually into the locomotive's tender. It was not until 1915 that the GER supplied a shelter for this work to be carried out. Modernisation of the facilities in the 1930s saw a mechanised coal plant supplied along with rationalisation of the works site and general (heavy) repairs ceased in 1934. The facilities of the old factory were still utilised by the engine shed for a number of years; the shed was coded 32A under British Railways. In an era when travel by rail was the only way for holiday-makers to travel, additional motive power and coaching stock was required in the summer months to cater for the volume of traffic on offer. The locomotives seen here are stored for the winter – No 64802, a Class J39, was built at Darlington in October 1930 and withdrawn in April 1961; Class J50 No 68899, built Doncaster in April 1914, withdrawn December 1960; and Class D16/3 No 62544, built Stratford Works in December 1903 with withdrawal in December 1959. *Dr Ian C Allen E3925*

Should a locomotive on a through working fail en-route then Norwich was well placed to 'fix the problem', LMS Class 4F No 44519 had failed at Great Yarmouth and was towed to the depot for repair – in this case the brick arch in the firebox had collapsed and required rebuilding. Above the locomotive is the sand plant; sand is dropped onto the railhead to aid adhesion under adverse conditions – leaves on the line – that is still a problem today. Under the coaling tower is No 65581, one of the depot's Class J17s. Dr Allen did not bother recording the number of the Brush Type 2, which would soon oust steam from the area. *Dr Ian C Allen M425*

2
West to Norwich

In 1880, Great Yarmouth's three main termini were completely isolated from each other and on 26th August of that year the Yarmouth Union Railway (YUR) was authorised in an attempt to remedy the situation. The YUR was a short line, just over a mile long, and went from a junction just outside Beach station, west across Caister Road, then due south back into the town following the backs of the houses in Alderson Road. It then went on to the street by the White Swan Inn and finally made a junction with the GER tramway line from Vauxhall station just east of the bridge over the Bure. The joint line then continued on to the principal quays alongside the Yare, these lines were worked by tramway locomotives that were kept at the GE locomotive shed at Vauxhall station when not in use. Throughout the whole life of the quayside lines the main traffic carried was 'salt and coal in and loose fish out' – scrap was also exported through the port in the 1960s when the railways were rationalised. The lines were finally abandoned during the 1970s and the bulk of them were lifted in 1985. In the summer of 1930 the LNER purchased two double-ended (cab at each end) Super Sentinel locomotives to work the Wisbech & Upwell Tramway. They were fitted with two-speed gearboxes and designed as tram locomotives with wheels and motion covered to operate in roadside locations. Both locomotives were later transferred to Yarmouth to work on the dockside tramway. LNER No 8403, then 8186 under the LNER's 1946's renumbering scheme, was allocated BR No 68186, although it was never carried as it was scrapped in February 1952 – some four years after Nationalisation. *Dr Ian C Allen E363*

The Bill for the Yarmouth & Norwich Railway (Y&NR) received Royal Assent on 18th June 1842. Work started on the line in April 1843 and the line and its stations were opened on 1st May 1844. The terminus was originally named Yarmouth Vauxhall. The Y&NR line to Norwich through Reedham was the first railway in the county to open. On 30th June 1845 a Bill authorising the amalgamation of the Y&NR with the Norwich & Brandon Railway came into effect and Yarmouth Vauxhall station became part of the Norfolk Railway (NR). The ECR took over the NR, including Yarmouth Vauxhall station, on 8th May 1848. By the 1860s the railways in East Anglia were in financial trouble, and most were leased to the Eastern Counties Railway, which wished to amalgamate formally but could not obtain government agreement for this until an Act of Parliament on 7th August 1862, when the GER was formed. However, Yarmouth Vauxhall became GER property on 1st July 1862 when it took over the ECR and the EUR before the Bill received the Royal Assent. Two decades later the GER started the new line about one mile west of Yarmouth Vauxhall and the junction was named Breydon. The first section of the new line opened on 1st March 1883 as far as Acle. During World War 2, in May 1943, the station was badly damaged during an air raid, resulting in the upper floor of the passenger station needing to be demolished. The remains of the original station building were removed, and the station rebuilt, in 1960. Before rail closures of the 1950s and the later Beeching 'axe' the station was the largest of three major railway stations in the town. Class E4 No 7501 was built in September 1896 as a member of the GER's 'T26' class. The 100 locomotives were designed for working cross-country services and those that survived into BR ownership were concentrated in Cambridgeshire and the Eastern Counties such as this view taken at Yarmouth (Vauxhall) sometime in the late 1920s and 1930s this would have been a typical scene with a mix of pre- and post-Grouping motive power and rolling stock. No 7501 was withdrawn in October 1938. *Dr Ian C Allen E550*

Top: Trains in this area carried route codes and the disc on the locomotive No 62586 indicates a Yarmouth to Norwich via Reedham working. The two locomotives in the siding would be waiting to take over the Lowestoft or Yarmouth through coaches of trains that divided at Reedham on summer Saturdays rather than add to the congestion at Norwich Thorpe. The original station was replaced on 1st June 1904 by a new one around a quarter of a mile to the west – it was renamed Reedham (Norfolk) in 1928 to avoid confusion with the Southern Railway station of Reedham Halt. The locomotive on the left, No 62511, an LNER Class D16/3, was built in April 1901, and withdrawn from Norwich Thorpe depot in December 1959. The train engine, No 62586, also a product of Stratford in May 1910, was withdrawn in March 1958, again from Norwich Thorpe. *Dr Ian C Allen E1038*

Bottom: Class L1 2-6-4T No 67717 runs into Reedham with a Lowestoft-Norwich service. The locomotive was constructed at Darlington in April 1948; initially allocated to Neasden depot it was reallocated to Lowestoft in March 1953, withdrawal occurred at Gorton in July 1961, after only 13 years service. In the adjacent siding Class F6 No 67226 waits to take over the Lowestoft section of a York-Yarmouth/Lowestoft service that will split here. *Dr Ian C Allen E2051*

Top: Taken from the Witton Green overbridge, the goods yard at Reedham is seen here with the station beyond the Ferry Road bridge. There are ongoing engineering works with new point work waiting to be laid. Class A5 No 69824 hauls a freight over track that has had the ballast removed with replacement sleepers alongside. The four box vans behind the locomotive would add to the train's braking ability as the open wagons would only have handbrakes. No 69824 was built at Gorton Works in April 1923 to a Great Central Railway order as a Class 9N; initially allocated to Neasden it was moved to Norwich Thorpe in May 1952. Reallocated to Lowestoft in October 1955 it left East Anglia in February 1957, being withdrawn from Lincoln depot in December 1958.
Dr Ian C Allen E3090

Middle: BR Standard Class 7MT 4-6-2 No 70006 *Robert Burns* was allocated to the Eastern Region following delivery from Crewe Works in April 1951 until transferred to the London Midland Region in November 1963. It is seen here running into Haddiscoe Low Level station at the head of an express service; the stations here were placed for operational reasons, rather than public convenience. The bridge carrying the High Level line can be seen behind the telegraph pole. The original station here was opened in 1847, but later closed by the GER in 1904 when the current one opened as Haddiscoe Low Level, on 9th May. Following rationalisation of railways in the area it lost its Low Level title when the High Level station closed on 2nd November 1959.
Dr Ian C Allen BR287

Bottom: Class L1 2-6-4T No 67786 hauls the morning papers train on the loop from the East Suffolk line to Haddiscoe Low Level station in the late 1950s. The Class L1 was a Thompson-design for the LNER, however No 67786 did not emerge from the works of Robert Stephenson & Hawthorn until April 1950. It was allocated to Yarmouth South Town from October 1957 – and reallocated to Norwich Thorpe in January 1959 until February 1960 – conveniently dating the image to this period.
Dr Ian C Allen E1134

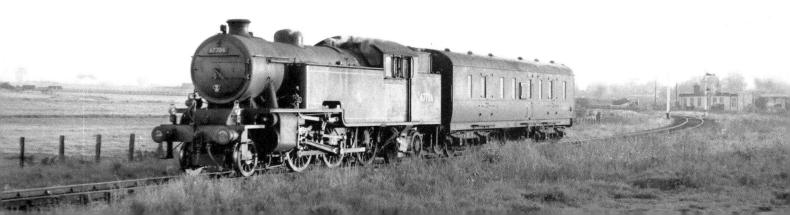

Top: No 62592 crosses to the north bank of the River Yare over Reedham swing bridge, on its journey from Lowestoft to Norwich, at the head of a stopping passenger train, consisting of pre-Nationalisation stock. At one time there was a southeast to northeast line enabling direct running from Lowestoft to Great Yarmouth without the need to reverse at Reedham station; the link was closed c1878. No 62592 emerged in July 1910 as GER Class D15 No 1801. It was twice rebuilt by the LNER, firstly in April 1929 as a 'D16/2' then again in June 1945 to a 'D16/3', in this case the decorative valancing over the driving wheels was retained. Withdrawal came on All Fools Day 1958. *Dr Ian C Allen E883*

Middle: Slightly more modern rolling stock is seen behind Class F6 No 67223 as the train crosses Reedham swing bridge; the leading vehicle is a BR-design Mk 1 Brake Corridor Second followed by an LNER-built Vestibule Restaurant Third complete with carriage boards. BR abolished Third Class travel on 3rd June 1956. Class F6, No 67226, was built in May 1911, as GER No 67 and withdrawn from Lowestoft Depot in November 1955. *Dr Ian C Allen E1620*

3

Wells, Wroxham
and Wymondham to Dereham

Top: Wells was first linked to the railway network when the Wells & Fakenham Railway (W&FR) opened the line to Fakenham. It was originally planned to have been opened on 1st June 1857, but negotiations with the ECR, which would operate the line, delayed it until 1st December 1857. The aim was that the railway would help reverse the declining fortunes of the town, whose inability to take ships of increasing size saw it overtaken by other ports. The decline continued despite the construction of a short line to Wells harbour in 1860; in 1862, the W&FR became part of the GER. The West Norfolk Junction Railway was the next to come to Wells, on 17th August 1866. The line came from Heacham on a single track aimed at exploiting the great arc of coastline between Hunstanton and Yarmouth. This line entered the town on a sharp curve, turning through a full 180 degrees before converging with the Wells & Fakenham branch from Dereham for the final approach. West Norfolk services used the outer face of a sheltered wooden island platform to the south of the station, with the inner face for services to Dereham and Wymondham. The Dereham side was unusual in that there was a platform on either side of the train, allowing the passengers the choice of which side to alight. Opened as Wells on 1st December 1857, it was renamed Wells-on-Sea on 1st July 1923; the final change to Wells-next-the-Sea occurred on 1st January 1957. The Heacham line closed to all traffic on 2nd June 1952 following severe flood damage to the route. The Dereham line closed to passenger traffic on 5th October 1964, followed by freight traffic on 2nd November. Class D16/3 No 62552, awaiting departure time, was built by the GER (as No 1841) in November 1906; allocated to Norwich Thorpe between June 1953 and June 1954, it survived until October 1955. Standing on what seems to be an adjacent platform, LNER Class J19 No 64642 is outside the goods shed; built in November 1912 it remained in service until April 1960. *Dr Ian C Allen E2321*

Opposite bottom: Although a GER design, No 62613 emerged in June 1923 as a Class D16; it was rebuilt as a 'D16/2' in May 1931, and again under BR auspices, in December 1948, as a D16/3 to the form illustrated. It is seen running into Brundall Junction station from Great Yarmouth via Acle – as indicated by the headcode discs. The station, opened by the Y&NR on 1st May 1844, was actually in the parish of Braydeston, but took its name from its larger neighbour. The railway occupied a narrow strip of land that necessitated the platforms being staggered. Withdrawal of No 62613 came in October 1960. *Dr Ian C Allen E1247*

Top: The depot at Wells was a sub-shed of Norwich and unusual in that it shared space with the goods shed (as seen in the previous image). No 65532, a member of Class J17, has turned on the 44ft 8in diameter turntable which in theory limited the length of locomotives that could be turned. There was actually a third side to the junction providing a direct link between the Heacham and Dereham lines that saw very limited use as a means to bypass the station, but could be used to turn longer locomotives. The open wagon, standing on a spur from the turntable, probably contained an emergency locomotive coal supply; although S. V. Varham, the local coal merchants, operated from the station with its office hidden behind the water tank. Water for the locomotives was obtained from a well, pumped by a steam engine until the early 1950s when electricity was substituted. *Dr Ian C Allen E1252*

Bottom: A number of halts were opened by the LNER in the early 1920s in an effort to increase traffic with minimum expenditure. Wighton Halt, opened on 1st February 1924, was a minimal affair with the platform at around a single coach length, and waiting shelter. Serving a population of around 500 the halt was unstaffed with no freight facilities. No 62608 was a member of the 'D16/3' class. Built in July 1911 as a member of GER Class H88 (No 1797), it was rebuilt into the form seen here in July 1937. It was allocated to Norwich for two periods in the 1950s – June/July 1951 and January 1952 to October 1955. It, like a number of locomotives, was reallocated to Cambridge before withdrawal in January 1957. *Dr Ian C Allen E3770*

Little and Great Walsingham have been places of religious pilgrimage dating back several hundred years – despite this a small station was sufficient throughout the life of the line. Following closure the station building has been extended and today serves as a Russian Orthodox Chapel. The GER introduced its Class G58 for freight working in 1900, with No 1217 leaving the Works in May 1905. As Class J17 No 65567, it is seen standing with its short freight train outside the goods shed at Walsingham, during its journey south to Norwich via Dereham. It was withdrawn in August 1962 and subsequently preserved; as part of the National Collection it is currently on static display at Barrow Hill Museum. *Dr Ian C Allen E1207*

Disproving the fact that Norfolk is flat, the gradient of the track behind the train is obvious. *Dr Ian C Allen E2116*

Top: The line between Wroxham and Broom Green junction, just to the north of County School station, opened in five stages between 8th January 1879 and 1st May 1882. Around the midway point was Aylsham, the line connecting eastwards to Wroxham opened on 1st January 1880. Renamed Aylsham (South) on 27th September 1948, closure to passenger traffic pre-dated the Beeching era, with services finishing on 15th September 1952; general goods traffic continued until 1st March 1977. However, this was not the end as the line remained open to serve Lenwade, via a new curve at Themelthorpe, that was on the former M&GNJt route to Norwich City station. With a short passenger train in tow Class E4 2-4-0 No 62792 waits to depart with a Wroxham service. It was built in June 1902 as a member of the GER's Class T26, numbered 1250; it was withdrawn in June 1956. Standing adjacent is Class J17 No 65513 (built November 1900 as GER Class G58). It was rebuilt by the LNER from a Class J16 by the fitting of a round top boiler in place of the original Belpaire type. *Dr Ian C Allen E724*

Bottom: Trains cross at Aylsham (South) with Class E4 2-4-0 No 62787 heading towards Wroxham. Built in January 1895 as GER Class T26, No 494, the locomotive was allocated to Norwich depot between August 1950 and August 1956, and was probably one of four sub-shedded at Dereham to work the semi-circular Dereham-County School-Wroxham-Norwich service. No 62787 was transferred to Cambridge before withdrawal in November 1956. The station site is now the western terminus, and headquarters, of the 15in (381mm) gauge Bure Valley Railway running to Wroxham alongside a public footpath on the original trackbed.
Dr Ian C Allen E834

Top: It's a winter's day as No 64674 waits at Foulsham to depart with a load of open wagons filled with sugar beet bound for one of Norfolk's processing facilities. For many years this traffic brought much needed revenue to several lines around the county. The signalman returns to his 'box having handed the single line token to the driver of No 64674; built in November 1920 it was the last member of the GER Class T22 (later 'J19') to be constructed. The station once boasted two 'boxes – East and West – which were replaced by the single structure seen here. During World War 2 the station served as the nearest railhead for the nearby RAF Foulsham, situated about a mile to the north of the station. The airfield opened in May 1942, although far from ready with its first squadrons not arriving until October. Postwar the airfield was passed to Care & Maintenance, remaining MoD property until the 1980s. The station lost its passenger traffic on 15th September 1952, with freight services eastwards to Reepham ceasing at the same date. Goods traffic westwards to County School remained until 31st October 1964. *Dr Ian C Allen E1111*

Bottom: Opened as plain Elmham in 1857 with the line, it was renamed as North Elmham on 1st September 1872. Equipped with a single passenger platform on the down line. with a goods loop alongside, the passing of passenger trains was not permitted. The LNER rebuilt the station with a simple brick building replacing the earlier timber framed building; it was the location for a rail served dairy, with daily milk trains operating from the station to Ilford. A shunting horse was used to move loaded milk wagons from the down to the up side of the line for collection. The dairy closed in October 1963, with passenger traffic ceasing north of Dereham on 5th October 1964, although public goods traffic continued until July 1971. No 65567 is seen at the head of a Railway Correspondence & Travel Society special on the return trip from Foulsham. The 'Great Eastern Commemorative Steam Rail Tour' ran on 31st March 1962; 'Britannia' No 70003 *John Bunyan* took the train from London Liverpool Street to Norwich Thorpe where No 65567 took over, running Norwich-Wymondham-Dereham-Foulsham-Dereham-Swaffham-Thetford, where No 70003 took over for the trip back to London. *Dr Ian C Allen E3043*

Top: The Lynn & Dereham Railway (L&DR) and the Norfolk Railway (NR) both obtained Parliament's permission to build lines to Dereham in 1845, at the height of the so-called 'Railway Mania'; a period when railways were being built across the whole country. The NR, building its line from Wymondham, reached Dereham first, and opened to passengers on 15th February 1847. The line from King's Lynn had to wait until 11th September 1848 when the L&DR built its own terminal station just before the junction with the NR. This was closed in 1850 when services were extended to the NR's station. The station was built in stages, being expanded over several decades. It was provided with four platforms, with northbound platforms 2 and 3 being set back to back. Platform 4 is a short bay platform and was originally dedicated for trains heading towards King's Lynn. Beeching's report intended to retain the King's Lynn-Dereham-Wymondham (for Norwich) line for express trains and freight. However, the line from King's Lynn was rationalised and subsequently closed in 1968, leaving a Dereham-Norwich service. After withdrawal of this remaining service on 6th October 1969 it remained open as a coal depot until 12th September 1984; fertiliser traffic to a private siding continued for a while longer. Freight trains continued to pass through the station to North Elmham until 1989. The now preserved Class B12/3 No 61572 stands in the Down platform whilst working a Yarmouth Vauxhall-Whitemoor perishables service sometime during 1960. Although this train could have used the avoiding line, if there was any trade to or from the town it was useful to make use of the service. In the platform Class J15 No 65469 is taking water before departing southwards with a milk train from North Elmham. The signalman has already pulled off the signal for its departure. *Dr Ian C Allen E3181*

Bottom: Class J17 No 65586 is seen at Dereham whilst shunting the extensive yards. The line curving off to the left was the south to east avoiding line enabling through services to bypass the station. No 65586 entered traffic in December 1910 as GER No 1236, being withdrawn from March depot in April 1962. *Dr Ian C Allen E3003*

Having collected additional traffic, a Lowestoft-Whitemoor freight is seen leaving Dereham for King's Lynn behind No 62524. Dating from March 1902, the locomotive was rebuilt as a Class D16/3 from a 'D14' in January 1930 and served the GER and its successors for 58 years. The shed, which can be seen behind the train, had a 45ft turntable, the triangle would have been used for turning longer locomotives. *Dr Ian C Allen E3506*

Travelling south from Dereham is Class D16/3 No 62511 hauling a short train of two milk tanks and bogie van from North Elmham. The locomotive was built at Stratford Works in April 1901, lasting until December 1959. The gas holder was at the town's works that opened on this site in 1885 under the ownership of the local authority; the derelict building is part of an iron works. *Dr Ian C Allen E3000*

Hunstanton to King's Lynn

Above: Heacham station opened with the King's Lynn-Hunstanton line on 3rd October 1862 and became the junction for the West Norfolk branch when it opened on 17th August 1866. The junction was immediately to the north of the station with services from Wells terminating in the bay platform rather than running direct to King's Lynn. LNER Class D16/3 No 62552 has arrived with its three-coach train prior to closure to passenger services on 31st May 1952. Freight, and occasional excursion traffic, continued on the West Norfolk branch, although the severe flooding of January 1953 dealt the route a body-blow; damage was so severe that BR decided not to repair the line between Holkham and Wells. The station, along with the line, closed on 5th May 1969, although freight traffic had terminated earlier on 28th December 1964. *Dr Ian C Allen E2316*

Opposite top: There was a level crossing at the southern end of the platforms at Heacham, so the gates had to be closed prior to trains from Hunstanton arriving at the station, no doubt to the annoyance of road traffic that was increasing during the postwar era. Class D15/2 No 62507 is fitted with a superheated Belpaire boiler with extended smokebox, unlike many of its contemporaries that acquired the round-top versions. One of the superheater anti-vacuum valves can be seen on the smokebox just behind the chimney. No 62507 was the only member of the class that had the decorative framing over the coupling rods removed, withdrawal came at King's Lynn in April 1952. On 28th November 2006, BR Mk 1 First Class Corridor coach No 13318 arrived for conversion to holiday accommodation; this and the former Waiting Rooms at the station are available as holiday lets. *Dr Ian C Allen E755*

Opposite bottom: As at Heacham the level crossing is to the immediate southern end of the platforms at Wolferton that are behind ICA as he took this image of Class D16/3 No 62539 arriving and collecting the single-line tablet for the section north to Heacham from the signalman. Built in October 1903 as GER No 1868, the locomotive was rebuilt as a Class D16/3 in September 1929. As can be seen when compared with the previous image it has received a round-topped boiler and had the decorative framing over the coupling rods removed. The station was well known as the nearest station to Sandringham House, and royal trains brought the Monarch and family to and from the estate until 1966. The station's facilities included a spacious carriage dock, ornate goods and coal storage buildings, along with a small gas works that provided sufficient gas to light the entire station. King's Lynn is now the nearest railhead for royals and visitors alike. After spending some time as a museum, the station is now preserved in private hands. The signal box and part of the station are Grade II* listed. *Dr Ian C Allen E1465*

Opposite top: Before arriving at King's Lynn station the line from Hunstanton (to the left) connected with the Dereham line (above the third carriage) at King's Lynn junction along with the lines from the south (above the second carriage) – to arrive in the town from an easterly direction. The junction also had connections to the Lynn Docks branch as well as the locomotive depot, making this a very busy location. Pulling its four-coach train off the Hunstanton line is No 69617, one of the first 20 locomotives of its type to be constructed – in this case in January 1924 – originally carrying Belpaire boilers, they were rebuilt with round-top boilers and reclassified by the LNER as Class N7/4. No 69617 was rebuilt in April 1944 and withdrawn from Stratford in July 1960. *Dr Ian C Allen E2227*

Opposite bottom: Class N7/4 No 69620 is seen north of King's Lynn junction on its way to Hunstanton with four BR Mk 1 carriages in tow; the postman is paying more attention to the photographer rather than the train – maybe ICA was blocking the footpath! The locomotive was built in February 1924; entering traffic as No 998E, it was allocated to King's Lynn between June 1958 and March 1959. *Dr Ian C Allen E2953*

This page top: With Tennyson Avenue bridge seen to the right, No 62588 heads past the 'box at King's Lynn junction whilst working a London Liverpool Street-Hunstanton stopping service. The train would have had to reverse in King's Lynn station where the Class D16/3 would have been attached for the journey along the coast. Entering service in June 1910, as GER No 1817, it was withdrawn from Cambridge in October 1958. *Dr Ian C Allen E3327*

This page bottom: 'Foreign' motive power passes King's Lynn junction as it heads out of town with a service for Peterborough. However, the LMS Class 4MT No 43089 was actually built at the LNER's Darlington Works in December 1950 and allocated to King's Lynn between November 1957 and November 1960. The locomotive was a regular sight in East Anglia, generally serving the Eastern Region from construction until it was finally reallocated to the London Midland Region in June 1964; withdrawal came in November 1965 from Langwith Junction depot. *Dr Ian C Allen M676*

5

Dereham to King's Lynn

Opposite top: Around the mid-point of the Dereham-King's Lynn line was Swaffham – the largest settlement and market town on the route. It was the junction for the line south to Thetford. Passenger services on the Thetford line ceased on 15th June 1964, the freight service continued as far south as Watton until 19th April 1965. Final closure for Swaffham station occurred on 9th September 1968 when passenger services between King's Lynn and Dereham ceased, freight traffic having been lost on 31st January 1966. Classes E4 No 62787 and C12 No 67367 double-head a three-coach train out of Swaffham on a school day service

to Thetford. This was to facilitate a crew change at Swaffham without leaving a locomotive unattended at Thetford for a number of hours. A single locomotive was sufficient to operate the basic service over the line to Thetford; however, a second locomotive was sent daily during term time from King's Lynn to operate the school train. The Class C12 4-4-2T was a Great Northern Railway design dating from 1898. No 67367 was built at Doncaster Works in May 1899 (as GNR No 1509), and shedded at King's Lynn between November 1953 and December 1955. It was withdrawn in August 1958. *Dr Ian C Allen E3215*

Opposite bottom: The original two-road shed at Swaffham was opened by the L&DR on 10th August 1847, and was reached from the 45ft turntable as it was built at an angle to the running lines. It was demolished by the LNER, being replaced by a servicing point – consisiting of the original water tank, coal stage and locomotive pit – that closed on 2nd April 1962 when all services were dieselised. Standing by the water tank, Nos 67360 and 62797 are being prepared for a school day trip to Thetford. *Dr Ian C Allen E1645*

This page top: Goods facilities were minimal at Middleton Towers, with the loading bay seen here and a siding with road access the other side of the level crossing. However, behind the photographer was the connection to a large sand quarry that still supplies the glass industry with the raw material. The leading locomotive, No 68498, was built to the GER's 'S56' class design in April 1890 as its No 336; it was allocated to King's Lynn between August 1953 and August 1958 – withdrawal came in August 1959. The other locomotive, a Class J20, was not identified, but would have been one of those allocated to March depot. As there was no run round loop, all traffic to the quarry would have required the use of two locomotives to enable wagons to be shunted within the exchange sidings. *Dr Ian C Allen E884*

This page bottom: LNER Class J19 No 64640 and an unidentified Class J69 double-head a sand train towards King's Lynn. Note the loading gauge, to the right of the telegraph pole, in the adjacent goods yard. Built at Stratford in November 1912, as the first member of the GER's Class T77, No 64640 was allocated to King's Lynn twice in the 1950s, January 1949 to March 1952 and May 1957 until withdrawn in November 1959. *Dr Ian C Allen E766*

6

King's Lynn to Ely and Newmarket

This page: An express service for Liverpool Street via Ely and Cambridge leaves King's Lynn hauled by Class B17/6 No 61642 *Kilverstone Hall*. Built at Darlington Works in May 1933, the locomotive was rebuilt to the form seen here in October 1954; allocated to Cambridge depot at Nationalisation it was withdrawn from there in September 1958. Kilverstone Hall is a country house built in the early 17th century that was passed down the Wright family of Kilverstone. It was greatly enlarged by Josiah Vavasseur, technical director of the arms manufacturing firm William Armstrong Ltd. It included a parkland estate of 3,000 acres. Upon Vavasseur's death in 1908 the house and park were inherited by Cecil Fisher, son of Admiral Lord Fisher and adopted heir to Vavasseur. Admiral Fisher and his wife moved into the Hall by invitation of Cecil Fisher upon the Admiral's retirement as First Sea Lord in 1910 and lived there until he was recalled, again as First Sea Lord, upon the outbreak of World War 1 in 1914. The house was remodelled in a Jacobean style in 1913 and remains the property of the Fisher family and has the mailed fist and trident of Lord Fisher's baronial crest on its gateposts. The house is Grade II listed on the National Heritage List for England. *Dr Ian C Allen E3499*

Opposite top: Class D16/3 No 62543 leads an express service out of King's Lynn past the locomotive depot. The depot was part of the Cambridge Locomotive District, the shed here being the second on the site, dating from 1871 when the station was remodelled. The depot had the usual facilities complete with a 45ft 7in turntable, however, by the late 1920s this was inadequate as locomotive lengths increased; in 1932 a turntable from the recently closed Berwick shed was installed, increasing the length to 52ft. The depot closed on 12th April 1959; although initially remaining intact, it was demolished the following year – a 'J17' doing the honours with a chain from its coupling hook to the shed side-wall. No 62543 was built in December 1903, as GER Class S46 No 1852; rebuilt to Class D16/3 in February 1949 it survived until October 1958. *Dr Ian C Allen E4150*

Opposite bottom: Class J69/1 No 68542 is seen shunting grain wagons on the King's Lynn docks branch. The image is taken from the Gaywood Road bridge looking towards the station. The buildings to the right are those of Alfred Dodman & Co's factory. Dating from 1854 the company was known for the boilers, engines and castings used in its main business, the manufacture of fairground machinery, and, in conjunction with Frederick Savage, the well-known 'gallopers'. In 1896 the company built two locomotives mainly using traction engine components, one, 0-4-2T *Gazelle*, from the Shropshire & Montgomeryshire Rly, is now preserved. The company ceased trading in the mid-1970s. The port infrastructure developed in the 19th century following the formation of a docks and railway company in 1865. This built the Alexandra Dock that was completed in 1869 and linked by rail in 1870. By 1876 over 500 ships were using the new dock each year. The larger Bentinck Dock with a length of 2,600ft (800m) was opened in 1883. The port has traditionally relied on exporting agricultural produce for the bulk of its traffic. The last train left the dock estate in May 1993. No 68542 dates from February 1892 and saw service at King's Lynn, or South Lynn, depots between December 1947 and August 1958. *Dr Ian C Allen E709*

The station at Denver opened with the line on 1st January 1847 as Denver Road Gate, being renamed as Denver on 25th October the same year. Its first closure came on 1st February 1870, only to reopen 15 years later on 1st July 1885. Closure to passenger traffic for the second time was on 22nd September 1930 – however freight services continued until 13th July 1964. The junction for the Stoke Ferry line leads off to the left of the image. Class J69/1 No 68566 is standing opposite the junction box with the driver and shunter (by the signal post) conversing. The locomotive was completed in December 1895 as a member of GER Class S56, numbered 390 and withdrawn from Stratford depot in September 1962. *Dr Ian C Allen E1098*

Despite the reduction of much of the network in the 1960s the railways in Ely are still an important interchange point between several routes in England. With Ely North junction located at Queen Adelaide (approximately 1.5 miles [2km]), north of the station. From here the electrified ex-GER London-King's Lynn double-track main line (marketed as the Fen Line) runs north to Downham Market and King's Lynn. Two non-electrified double-track lines branch at North junction: the line to Norwich (marketed as the Breckland Line) diverges to the northeast; the line to March and Peterborough diverges to the northwest. Immediately east of Ely North junction is Potter Distribution Depot that has substantial railfreight facilities, whilst Cemex operates an asphalt and building materials depot at the site. Class D16/3 No 62518 entered trafffic in June 1901 as GER No 1887, being rebuilt to the form seen here in August 1943. It spent the first four years of its BR career allocated to Cambridge, moving to King's Lynn in March 1952 before withdrawal in October 1958. The four-wheel horsebox, No M42583, was an LMS design dating from 1948; all these vehicles had accommodation for the groom to travel. With the transport of racehorses moving to road transport the vehicles were withdrawn between December 1963 and March 1966. *Dr Ian C Allen E3324*

North Country Continental.

Express services from Liverpool/Manchester to Parkestone Quay were unofficially called the North Country Continental, enabling passsengers to catch ferry services to Europe. Running via various routes for ease of operation the train is seen between Ely and Fordham behind Class B17/6 No 61620 *Clumber*. Built at Darlington Works in November 1930 it was shedded at March depot between October 1952 and April 1959, from where it would have taken over the train, and withdrawn in January 1960 from King's Lynn. The locomotive is named after a country park in The Dukeries near Worksop in Nottinghamshire, England. The estate was the seat of the Pelham-Clintons, Dukes of Newcastle, being purchased by the National Trust in 1946. It is now listed Grade I on the Register of Historic Parks & Gardens. The main house was demolished in 1938 after damage by a series of fires. The nearby Grade I listed chapel in Gothic Revival style and a four-acre walled kitchen garden still survive. The gardens and the estate are managed by the National Trust and are open to the public all year round. *Dr Ian C Allen E1131*

The same service is seen after passing Barway crossing, between Ely and Soham, this time double-headed by Class K3/2 No 61949 and BR Class 7MT No 70030 *William Wordsworth*. Beyond the crossing was Barway Siding (shown on some maps as Barraway Siding) that closed on 13th July 1964 – there was never a station at this location. The 'K3' was built by NBL in September 1934, allocated to Norwich Thorpe between January 1959 and December 1960; it was withdrawn from Doncaster shed in April 1962. No 70030 was built at Crewe Works in November 1952, initially allocated to Holyhead it moved to East Anglia in July 1953, reallocated away in July 1963 and withdrawn from Carlisle Upperby depot in June 1966. *Dr Ian C Allen E1666*

7

Magdalen Road to Wisbech

Above: The sand trains from Middleton Towers were heavy and often required the use of two brake vans as the majority of open wagons during this period only had hand brakes, such a working is seen here near Wiggenhall Siding on the Magdalen Road-March line. No 64672 was built in October 1920 as a member of GER Class T77 – later Class J19. Shedded at March for much of the 1950s it was withdrawn in January 1959. *Dr Ian C Allen E1129*

Bottom: It was the ECR that first reached Wisbech from the south in May 1847 with the opening of a line from St Ives via March; a temporary wooden station named Wisbeach was built on the site of the future Wisbech goods yard. The East Anglian Railways (EAR) made its way from the east to Wisbech the following year with a line from Magdalen Road station; their station – on the site of the future Wisbech East station – was also a temporary structure named Wisbeach. A short curve joined the two lines. The two stations remained in use until at least 1851 when a lease was agreed between the two companies giving the operation of the EAR to the ECR, the agreement taking effect at the beginning of 1852. In 1862, the GER acquired the line and subsequently closed the ECR's Wisbeach station to passenger traffic the following year. A line from the station to the harbour was laid in 1863.
The renaming to Wisbech occurred on 4th May 1877. The station closed in 1968 and no trace of it remains today. A freight-only line remained extant as far as a factory based in the station's former goods yard; the old Wisbech East goods yard was acquired by Nestlé Purina from Railtrack in 1995 and was last used in 2000. Class D16/3 No 62513 leaves Wisbech East station bound for March. Constructed in May 1901 it was rebuilt to the form seen here in September 1948 and survived for another 10 years, being withdrawn in November 1958. *Dr Ian C Allen E3914*

The ECR obtained powers to construct a branch from Wisbech station to the harbour in 1852; however, it was not until 1862 that the first train was operated over the branch now owned by the GER. By the late 19th century Wisbech was one of the largest timber importers on the east coast with English Bros and J. T. Stanton & Co operating from the harbour. Class J15 No 65474 is not far from its home shed of March when seen on the Wisbech East Harbour branch, alongside the River Nene, in the late 1950s. Across the river the former M&GN line had a docks branch. The East Harbour line closed in 1966. No 65474 emerged from Stratford Works as No 546 of the GER's 'T77' class in July 1913, and was withdrawn in February 1960. *Dr Ian C Allen E1142*

The first proposals for a line from Wisbech, alongside the Wisbech Canal, and Well Creek to Upwell came in 1873; but, as with a lot of schemes, lack of finance caused the plan to fail. A second scheme in 1880 made use of the 1870 Tramways Act, enabling lines to be constructed with less stringent regulations, and therefore less expense. Services to Outwell village commenced on 20th August 1883, with the extension to Upwell following on 8th September 1884. There were proposals to extend to Welney but these came to nothing. The 1880 Act limited speed on the mainly roadside route to 8mph and the locomotive's motion had to be covered, along with 'cow-catchers, to protect the public. Passenger services were withdrawn on 31st December 1927, freight traffic continued until 23rd May 1966. Class J70 No 68217 pulls a rake of empty stock into Elm Bridge Depot early in the post Nationalisation period. *Dr Ian C Allen E2572*

8

Swaffham to Roundham Jct.

Left: The school day, double-headed Swaffham-Thetford service must have been a favourite of ICA's as he photographed it on a number of occasions. Class D16/3 No 62514 is seen double-heading with an Class J15 0-6-0 just outside Swaffham on the way to Watton. Swaffham station's outer distant signal can just be made out by the overbridge. No 62514 was built as a GER Class S46 in May 1901, and rebuilt as a 'D16/3' in May 1943, surviving until March 1957. *Dr Ian C Allen E3262*

Bottom: The first station on the Swaffham-Roudham junction line was at Holme Hale, which was once described as a 'scattered village', although it was probably nearer North Pickenham. The nearby World War 2 airfield was occupied by the Americans with the 491st and 492nd Bomb Groups being resident at some time – the small size of the station goods yard meant that most incoming traffic would have been dealt with at Swaffham. Postwar the airfield was used to site a trio of Thor Intermediate Range Ballistic Missiles; it has since reverted mostly to agriculture plus turkey farming, a wind farm and light industry occuping the former airfield. Class C12 No 67367 departs with a southbound service. The line closed to passenger services on 15th June 1964 with freight following on 19th April 1965. The station building, signal box and goods shed survive in private ownership. *Dr Ian C Allen E1086*

Top: The cleaners have seen that Class B12/3 No 61572 makes a fine sight as it heads a school excursion near Stow Bedon on 16th May 1961. The train ran from Swaffham and Thetford to London Liverpool Street. Built by Beyer, Peacock in August 1928 as LNER No 8572 to the GER Class S69 design dating from 1911, it was rebuilt to its current form a few years later. It was preserved by the M&GNJt Railway Society following its withdrawal in September 1961 – and can be seen in operation on the North Norfolk Railway.
Dr Ian C Allen E1220

Bottom: Steam-hauled passenger services along the line ceased in 1955 when DMUs took over, although steam haulage could still be seen on some occasions. Closure to passenger services has occurred at Stow Bedon station with the nameboard removed for resale – or the bonfire. Following demolition in the 1970s, the station site now serves as a car park for those wishing to explore the eight-mile circular walk of the Great Eastern Pingo Trail.
Dr Ian C Allen E1759

9

Yarmouth and Lowestoft to Beccles

Above: Yarmouth South Town station was the northern end of the East Suffolk Railway that opened on 1st June 1859 linking Ipswich with Yarmouth. From opening the line was operated by the ECR; amalgamation to form the GER occurred in 1862. During this period of operation there were express services to Liverpool Street (generally calling at Beccles where carriages from Lowestoft were added) and then other main stations and an all stations service to Beccles and Halesworth. In 1872 the addition of a curve at Haddiscoe High Level allowed a direct all stations service to run to Lowestoft – although this closed in 1934 as services could use the more direct Norfolk & Suffolk Joint (N&SJt) line along the coast, seen leading off to the right, serving Gorleston and Hopton on the way to Lowestoft Central. BR Standard Class 7MT No 70007 Coeur-de-Lion is departing Yarmouth South Town in September 1958 with an express for London Liverpool Street. The introduction of the 'Britannias' to the Great Eastern lines 'revolutionised' the services as for the first time the crews had locomotives that could handle the heavy traffic of the 1950s. No 70007 was allocated to Stratford depot when new; relocating to Norwich Thorpe a month later, it worked on the GE lines in the area for 10 years before being moved to March in November 1961. *Dr Ian C Allen BR36*

Opposite top: On 19th April 1959 the 9.55am Yarmouth South Town-Liverpool Street express is seen near North Gorleston junction heading for London. The service was known for having a buffet car, in this case the fourth vehicle behind the locomotive. Class B17/6 No 61664 was built by Robert Stephenson & Hawthorn in January 1937 as a Class B17/4; being rebuilt to the form seen here in February 1948. It was allocated to either Norwich Thorpe or Yarmouth South Town for much of its BR career. 23 of the class were named after football clubs with No 61664 becoming *Liverpool*. The bridge to the left of the locomotive took the former N&SJt line from the junction, over Breydon Water, round to Caister Road junction. This section of line closed in 1953. Passenger services to Yarmouth South Town ended on 4th May 1970 when the line south to Lowestoft closed. *Dr Ian C Allen E2179*

Opposite bottom: It was common practice for locomotives to be placed into store during quiet times of the year and a trio of Class D16/3s are seen stored at Yarmouth South Town. Nos 62670, 62604 and 62613 have sacking tied around their chimneys to prevent water ingress. No 62613 sports the 1956 BR crest with the others retaining the original version. *Dr Ian C Allen E1994*

Opposite top: There were two swing bridges over the River Waveney, the first out of Yarmouth South Town was at St Olaves. The line saw little investment during the 86-year period of GER and LNER ownership, and the cost of maintaining the Yarmouth to Beccles line to express standards for the benefit of holiday traffic became prohibitive, especially once Breydon Viaduct, connecting Yarmouth Beach with Yarmouth South Town, closed in 1953 which led to the direct line between Yarmouth and Lowestoft becoming underused. The first of the BR Standard locomotives was Class 7MT No 70000 *Britannia* that left Crewe Works in January 1951. Allocated to Stratford depot when new, reallocation to Norwich Thorpe came in January 1959, before transfer to the London Midland Region at Willesden in March 1963. No 70000 is seen here having crossed the swing bridge bound for Yarmouth South Town.
Dr Ian C Allen BR259

Opposite bottom: Double-headed Class B17/6s head north through Aldeby station and past the signal box en route to Yarmouth South Town, with No 61656 *Leeds United* at the head of the express service from London Liverpool Street. Built at Darlington Works in May 1936 as a Class B17/4 it was rebuilt with a round top boiler in November 1953. Allocated to Yarmouth South Town between January 1955 and September 1959 either side of periods at Norwich Thorpe depot. Aldeby, located on the Beccles-Yarmouth South Town line, was opened to traffic by the East Suffolk Railway on 4th December 1854. It closed to passengers on 2nd November 1959 and freight on 28th December 1964. *Dr Ian C Allen E2911*

This page, top: Class F6s double-head this stopping passenger service on the approach to Lowestoft Central having just passed Coke Ovens junction. The name originates from 1847 when coke ovens provided fuel from the arrival of the first railway until the late 1880s. Dating from the 1894-1901 period the 20 engines of GER Class G69 were all constructed at Stratford Works, with the train engine, No 67226, emerging as GER No 67 in May 1911; the leading locomotive cannot be clearly identified but may well be 67234. *Dr Ian C Allen E6390*

This page bottom: Having left Lowestoft Central, on the north side of Lake Lothing, Class F6 (GER Class G69) No 67223 approaches Coke Ovens junction with its two-coach stopping service. The junction was the southern end of the N&SJt line running along the coast to Great Yarmouth. Opened as Lowestoft on 1st July 1847 the addition of Central came on 1st October 1903 soon after the N&SJt opened (to avoid confusion with the latter's Lowestoft North); losing the suffix after the N&SJt closed on 2nd May 1970.
Dr Ian C Allen E3097

41

Top: The first shed at Lowestoft was a two-road brick structure on the north side of the station with a turntable on a separate spur. It was located close to Denmark Road on the site of what was later the goods shed. The shed could only accommodate four locomotives and attracted complaints from local residents due to smoke emissions. A new four-road shed was built in 1882 at a cost of £5,650 on the north shore of Lake Lothing beyond what later became Coke Ovens junction. The turntable was initially on a single spur alongside the yard but it was replaced by a 65ft (20m) version and repositioned at the western boundary of the yard, seen to the right of Class D16/3 No 62517. Built in June 1901 the locomotive was shedded at Lowestoft from January to April 1954. Allocated to all three Yarmouth sheds – Beach, South Town and Vauxhall at various times - it would have been a regular visitor. Withdrawal came from March depot in September 1959. In the 1930s, new coal handling and water softening plants were installed. Coded 32C by BR, the shed was officially closed in September 1960, although visiting locomotives continued to use the shed until it reportedly 'closed completely' on 8th July 1962. The shed served as a cattle quarantine station for a number of years before demolition in 1983. *Dr Ian C Allen E4180*

Bottom: Branded 'Civil Engineer Departmental Locomotive No 38' the locomotive, seen here on Lowestoft Quay duties, entered traffic in September 1930 as Class Y3 No 61 (later 8168), one of 32 built by Sentinel (Shrewsbury) Ltd. It never carried its allocated BR number, along with 10 class members that were either withdrawn early in BR days or transferred to departmental stock. Transferred to Departmental stock in May 1953 it continued to work the quayside lines until February 1959. Something interesting must be taking place at the shop of Walter Regis at the junction of Station Square and Waveney Road on the road tramway section to the harbour. *Dr Ian C Allen E4190*

Top: To the east of Oulton Broad North junction was Lowestoft Sleeper Depot, home for two Sentinel vertical-boilered locomotives – latterly Departmental Nos 7 and 41 were the resident motive power. The baulks of timber laid alongside the track were for the storage of pre-cut sleepers whilst awaiting 'pickling'. This involved placing the timber in specialised cylinders and using a vacuum to draw the heated creosote into the wood (see *Railway Bylines*, vol 3, issue 3 for a history of the works and process). No 7 was purchased by Kings of Norwich following withdrawal in May 1964 and recycled alongside Southern and Great Western locomotives. *Dr Ian C Allen E2476*

Bottom: With the pedestrian footbridge providing a connection between Denmark Road and Commercial Road, it also served as a suitable viewing gallery of the goods yard – although in this case ICA has access to the yard. No 67195 stands at the head of a rake of box vans alongside one of the loading platforms. The Class F5 was built in November 1904 as GER No 782 and spent two periods allocated to Lowestoft depot – October 1952-September 1954 and December 1954-December 1956; withdrawal occured at Stratford depot in May 1958. *Dr Ian C Allen E3166*

Opposite top: Class F6 No 67224 takes the Beccles line at Oulton Broad North junction that was to the east of the station. Alongside the line here were the premises of J. W. Brooke & Co Ltd, the company was founded in 1874 as a foundry and expanded into boat- and ship-building in the 1900s. Until 1913 it produced engines and motorcars (under the Brooke marque, between 1902 and 1913), and sub-contracted its boat building operations to another firm in Oulton Broad. In 1911 it opened a shipyard on the north side of Lake Lothing and began to produce its own craft, all using engines produced at its Adrian Works in the town. When car production ceased the company continued producing engines until 1938, totalling more than 7,000. It constructed boats and small ships for civilian and commercial use, as well as minor warships for the Royal Navy, Royal Navy of Oman, Royal Australian Navy,

Kenyan Navy and United States Navy. In 1914 it built a passenger motor boat for the Leopoldina Railway to carry up to 100 passengers across the harbour of Rio de Janeiro. *Dr Ian C Allen E3340*

Opposite bottom: The Oulton Broad swing bridge is on the seaward side of the Oulton Broad lock. The current bridge was installed in 1907, replacing a timber version installed in the late 1840s to carry a single railway track across the waterway. This is the smallest of the three swing bridges, with a different structure and operating system. Rather than being cable-hauled, the slewing movement for this bridge is achieved by a rack and pinion mechanism, driven from a machinery house mounted to one side of the slewing bridge structure. A single red flag being flown indicates that the bridge is working and in service; two red flags would indicate it is not working, although hopefully open for rail traffic. *Dr Ian C Allen E3515*

Top: Some trains coming off the South Side freight only line south of Lowestoft's inner harbour had a brake van at both ends, as the locomotive had to run round at Oulton Broad South before heading north over the swing bridge to gain access to the yards at Lowestoft. Here trains would be marshalled before departing for their final destinations. Class J15 No 65478 left the works in September 1913, as GER No 550, and spent most of the 1950s allocated to Lowestoft depot; transferred to Ipswich in March 1959, withdrawal occurred at Cambridge in October 1961. *Dr Ian C Allen E2011*

Bottom: Although allocated to East Anglian sheds through the 1950s the Class K3 2-6-0s are not usually associated with the area – at least not by photographers, although ICA appears to be an exception! No 61958 is seen here on the Lowestoft South Side line, just to the east of Oulton Broad South, as it prepares to take over the train; its allocation to this duty has attracted the attention of a number of local enthusiasts. The 'K3' was built by the NBL and was allocated at Yarmouth South Town before relocating to Lowestoft in November 1947, before moving to the former Great Central Railway depot at Staveley in March 1960. *Dr Ian C Allen E2513*

Top: Although the locomotive is the same as in the previous image the make up differs, and having taken over the service, Class K3/2 No 61958 is seen at Oulton Broad South junction, running off the South Side branch with some London-bound fish traffic. Alongside is Class J15 No 65478 that had brought in the train for the 'K3' to take south. The line to the left led to the swing bridge and the north side of Lake Lothing. *Dr Ian C Allen E1402*

Bottom: The second swing bridge over the River Waveney was at Beccles where Class B1 No 61300 is seen crossing it with a stopping passenger service; the locomotive was built by NBL in March 1948. The class was notable for being fitted with a steam-driven dynamo for powering the headcode lamps – although in daylight normal discs, or white-painted lamps, had to be shown. Upon withdrawal from the main line in November 1963 it was transferred to Departmental Stock – as No 23 – for use as a stationary boiler for train heating purposes, the drawhooks being removed to preclude use as a normal locomotive. *Dr Ian C Allen E4100*

10

Waverney Valley Line

The Waveney Valley line was a cross-country route running between Tivetshall in Norfolk to Beccles in Suffolk. The line was authorised by the Waveney Valley Railway Act of 3rd July 1851. The line opened in stages, firstly from Tivetshall to Harleston on 1st December 1855, then to Bungay on 2nd November 1860, and finally to Beccles. Lack of passengers saw the loss of services on 5th January 1953, with the last passenger train from Tivetshall junction to Beccles pulled by Class F3 No 67128. To reduce operating costs for the remaining freight traffic a Light Railway Order was obtained in November 1954. From 1960 the line was split into sections – Tivetshall to Harleston and Beccles to Bungay – with the centre portion totally closed. The remaining sections were finally closed from 19th April 1966 following the Beeching Report. Some of the last wagonloads to leave Ditchingham were sand and gravel from Broome Heath, used in the construction of Hammersmith fly-over in west London. In the early 1980s, many of the remaining old buildings on the eastern section, including stations and goods yards, were demolished to make way for realignment of the A143 – imaginatively named 'Old Railway Road'. The Class B12/3s were occasionally used on the line, but could not be used between Beccles and Bungay due to weight restrictions, so No 61535 would have worked in from Tivetshall. It had brought in the Ipswich breakdown crane to assist in the clearance of felled timber from the yard at Bungay during 1952 – many trees having succumbed during the recent gales with some blocking the line. No 61535 was allocated to Ipswich depot between August 1950 and November 1959 when it was withdrawn. *Dr Ian C Allen E2135*

Right: Class J15 No 65435 is seen in the yard at Bungay awaiting departure tender first towards Tivetshall. This view was taken from Outney Road overbridge that separated the goods yard from the station, this provided public access to Outney Common where there was a golf course and racecourse. The last race meeting took place on Monday 29th May 1939, with the Eastern Counties Open Hunters Chase being the final one, being won by El Raljo ridden by Mr F. Barclay. The locomotive was allocated to Lowestoft between February 1948 and August 1955. Reallocated to Ipswich in August 1955, it was withdrawn in October 1956.
Dr Ian C Allen E1593

Another view from the overbridge, with the entire goods yard illustrated looking east. Standing outside the signal box is Class J15 No 65433; dating from May 1911, it is handling a freight service whilst alongside, Class B12/3 No 61577 has brought in the Ipswich breakdown crane to assist with timber handling; loaded wagons are in evidence. Level crossing gates are over the northern extension of Broad Street, access to the goods yard being through almost identical gates just to the left of the crane's raised jib. *Dr Ian C Allen E2128*

Taken shortly before closure, Class J15 No 65471 leaves Homersfield yard whilst operating a goods service to Beccles, the quality of coal in the tender would seem to leave a bit to be desired so it's handy that a cab sheet has been fitted to protect the crew when working tender first. Following closure to passenger traffic, and the granting of the Light Railway Order, the signal box has been removed with the points controlled by levers, a ground frame can be seen just to the left of the tender. During World War 2 the station served Hardwick airfield some four miles away, with numerous American airmen using the station. The 93rd Bomb Group was in residence from December 1942 playing a prominent part in the war with a total of 396 operations, more than any other in the Eighth Air Force Bomb Group. *Dr Ian C Allen E2560*

Top: The crew of Class F4 No 67167 appear to be preparing to bale out as it passes the cameraman on the way to Tivetshall. The second coach is a Great Central Railway Vestibule Open Van Third Corridor dating from 1910, one of only five remaining in service in the mid-1950s. Dating from September 1908, No 67167 survived in traffic until September 1952. *Dr Ian C Allen E825*

Bottom: Any unusual visitors to the branch usually indicated the non-availability of the booked 0-6-0 tender locomotive at Norwich; in this case Class N7/3 0-6-2T No 69708 has deputised and is seen shunting the yard at Harleston on a frosty morning. The locomotive was built at Doncaster works in December 1927, spending much of its BR career allocated to Norfolk depots. The locomotive still carries its single line token catcher (on the lower side of the cab) from its short period allocated to Melton Constable shed – December 1950 to October 1951 – before relocating to Norwich Thorpe. Thomas Moy Ltd was a coal merchants who had a number of 'private owner' wagons prior to Nationalisation, including three on the 3ft gauge Southwold Railway. *Dr Ian C Allen E1573*

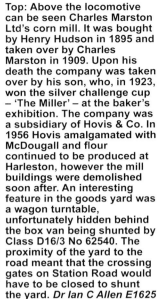

Top: Above the locomotive can be seen Charles Marston Ltd's corn mill. It was bought by Henry Hudson in 1895 and taken over by Charles Marston in 1909. Upon his death the company was taken over by his son, who, in 1923, won the silver challenge cup – 'The Miller' – at the baker's exhibition. The company was a subsidiary of Hovis & Co. In 1956 Hovis amalgamated with McDougall and flour continued to be produced at Harleston, however the mill buildings were demolished soon after. An interesting feature in the goods yard was a wagon turntable, unfortunately hidden behind the box van being shunted by Class D16/3 No 62540. The proximity of the yard to the road meant that the crossing gates on Station Road would have to be closed to shunt the yard. *Dr Ian C Allen E1625*

Middle: Class F4 No 67186 and train are seen passing the junction of the airfield branch at Pulham sometime before the summer of 1953. Land for the development of airship operations was acquired in 1913 with the base opening in February 1916. During the 1930s RAF expansion period the site was developed as a storage facility for ammunition, fuses and pyrotechnics. The former airship storage shed was used for filling practice bombs until it was hit in an air raid in 1940. With limited siding space available some traffic had to be handled at Harleston, Pulham St Mary and Tivetshall stations. The section of the branch remained in use until closure of the base on 1st February 1958; the locomotive however had already been withdrawn from Lowestoft in July 1951. *Dr Ian C Allen E1456*

Bottom: On 21st May 1960 the M&GNJR Society ran the 'Waveney Valley and M&GN Special'; hauling six coaches, Class J15 No 65469 ran from Norwich City, via Sheringham, Cromer junction, North Walsham and Trowse down to Tivetshall (where it is seen) then along the Waveney Valley line to Beccles. The locomotive was ailing at this point and classmate No 65462 double-headed the train from Beccles to Lowestoft Central from where No 65469 took the train back to Norwich Thorpe. *Dr Ian C Allen E3475*

11

Norwich Victoria to Ipswich

Top: What was to become Norwich Victoria station was opened by the Eastern Union Railway on 12th December 1849. Inconveniently located for traffic to the north of the county, a link opened on 8th September 1851 from the EUR line to the Norwich-Ely line, and most Ipswich services were transferred to Thorpe station. Left with just four or five trains each day Norwich Victoria closed to passenger traffic on 22nd May 1916. However, freight traffic continued to use the station site that became a general goods depot until closure on 31st January 1966. Coal traffic continued for another 20 years with the concentration depot and branch finally closing in September 1986. Class J67/1 No 68516, one of Holden's 'R24' design of 0-6-0T dating from December 1890, runs into Norwich Victoria past the original coal depot; although there are five 'Presflo' Blue Circle cement wagons in evidence. No 68516 was only fitted with a locomotive brake and therefore unable to operate fitted freight or passenger trains. *Dr Ian C Allen E2618*

Bottom: Taken from the Barrett Road overbridge Class J69/1 No 68555 is seen banking a Whitemoor-Norwich Victoria service towards the goods station – note the footplate crew's bicycles being taken for a ride. The train locomotive is BR Standard Class 7MT No 70013 *Oliver Cromwell*; classified as mixed traffic locomotives the 'Britannias' were just at home on freight as on passenger services. Dating from October 1895, No 68555 was allocated to Norwich Thorpe between March 1956 and February 1958 dating the image to this period. The trackbed here is now the Lakenham Way footpath. *Dr Ian C Allen E1176*

Top: The station at Diss was proposed by the Ipswich & Bury Railway, as part of their route to Norwich. Such were the changes in the railway industry that, in 1847, the Ipswich & Bury Railway became part of the EUR. The station at Diss opened on 2nd July 1849. The EUR became part of the ECR in 1854, until amalgamating with several other companies in 1862 to form the GER. Interestingly some goods shunting at Diss was carried out by horses as late as 1959. Class K3/2 No 61957 runs into Diss with a mixed collection of coaches in tow whilst operating a stopping passenger service from Norwich to Ipswich. Built by the NBL in November 1935, No 61957 spent its BR career allocated to East Anglian depots until reallocated to Colwick in December 1960, withdrawal coming less than two years later. *Dr Ian C Allen E3337*

Bottom: Although not steam powered – and there's a Class 31 in the background – scenes of early track measurement equipment are rare. British Railways bought a total of 13 of these trolleys from Matisa of Switzerland between 1957 and 1967. It was called Neptune, and this explains the devices emblazoned on the doors and at each end of the vehicle. The name was somewhat contrived from *North Eastern Electronic Peak Tracing Unit and Numerical Evaluator*. At the time of writing – www.teignrail.co.uk/neptune.php – gives full details of the vehicle. *Dr Ian C Allen MISC061*

In the 1840s, the town leaders of Eye unsuccessfully lobbied to have the new main line from London to Norwich run through Eye – instead, the line was routed through nearby Diss – which had an enormous effect on the prosperity and growth of the town. The town got its own station, on a later branch line, built by the Mellis & Eye Railway, opening on 2nd April 1867. It was closed to passengers on 2nd February 1931 and to goods on 13th July 1964. Class J17 No 65553 shunts the goods yard with the footplate crew and goods manager posing for their photograph to be taken; it was allocated to Norwich Thorpe from November 1949 until withdrawal almost 10 years later. *Dr Ian C Allen E1081*

Fellow class member No 65542 shunts the yard; built in September 1902 as GER No 1192 it was rebuilt to 'J17' specification in August 1923. Withdrawal came in May 1959 whilst allocated to Norwich Thorpe. The station and goods yard are now an industrial estate.
Dr Ian C Allen E1262

The station at Mellis opened when services commenced between Haughley and Burston on 2nd July 1849. The branch to Eye was served by a single platform that curved away from the main line; passenger trains started their journeys here until services ceased on 2nd February 1931. There were a number of goods sidings on the eastern side of the station connected with the operation of the branch. A goods shed was built on the western side of the line, where a corn mill and maltings were served by rail. Class J17 No 65542 is bringing a pick-up goods in from Eye, whilst a Norwich-Ipswich service leaves the adjacent platform formed with a two-car Metropolitan-Cammel lightweight DMU. The station lost its freight services on 28th December 1964; passenger services survived until 7th November 1966 when local services between Ipswich and Norwich were withdrawn. *Dr Ian C Allen E1936*

Class D16/3 No 62615 has brought a Suffolk Hunt special into Mellis Junction, behind the Vestibule Brake Coach are a number of horse boxes. As the train was carrying livestock it would be designated as a Class C freight as shown by the head code discs. The carriage of horses was once a source of valuable income for the railway as they would need to be transported from their home stables around the country. The locomotive retained its decorative valance over the driving wheels when it was rebuilt to Class D16/3 specification in April 1947; withdrawal came in December 1958. *Dr Ian C Allen E303*

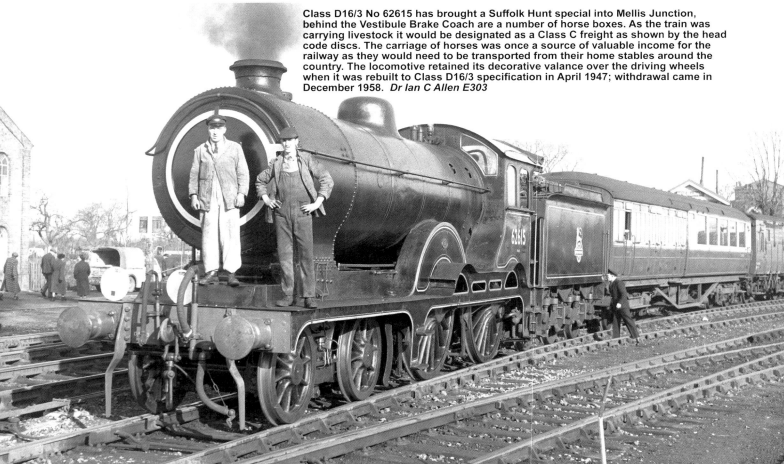

On 8th September 1956 the Norfolk Railway Society operated a railtour that ran a circular trip from Norwich Thorpe using Class E4 No 62797, one of 18 survivors to enter BR stock at Nationalisation. It is seen at Mellis Junction on the return trip from Eye with BR Standard Class 7MT No 70006 *Robert Burns* operating a Norwich-London Liverpool Street express service with a somewhat mixed selection of carriages. No 62797 was withdrawn from Cambridge depot in March 1958; No 70006 was transferred to the London Midland Region from March in November 1963. *Dr Ian C Allen BR162*

The special is seen preparing to depart for Eye earlier in the day; there was no top headcode bracket on the tender so the headboard remained on the smokebox, the coaching stock was far more uniform than the main line service seen in the earlier image. The building above the leading carriage is the malthouse that was served by a siding on the west side of the station. *Dr Ian C Allen E2802*

Mid-Suffolk Light Railway

Above: The Mid-Suffolk Light Railway (MSLR) was promoted as a result of the Light Railways Act of 1896 to alleviate the agricultural depression in Suffolk. The scheme was to connect the GER at Haughley and Halesworth, with a branch from Kenton to the outskirts of Ipswich at Westerfield. As with so many schemes promoted under the Light Railway Act, finance was short; the line from Haughley got as far as Laxfield, and the Kenton extension ended just a mile or so to the south. A goods-only service commenced on 20th September 1904; however, passengers had to wait until 29th September 1908 for the opportunity to legally travel! With the company in debt it initially survived the Grouping, but not for long as the LNER reluctantly took over the line on 1st July 1924, with the official transfer back dated to 1st January 1923. During World War 2 the line assumed some strategic importance as a supply route to the United States airfields at Mendlesham and Horam – initially for construction material, then men and munitions. The first half-mile from Haughley was relaid so heavier locomotives could be used – including USA Class S160 2-8-0s on munition trains up the 1 in 42 gradient. Nationalisation initially saw little change, but the end was nearing with the line closing completely on 28th July 1952. Readers wishing for a full history of the line are directed to Peter Paye's *The Mid-Suffolk Light Railway* (details in the bibliography). The end of the line was originally two miles past Laxfield Mill to Catfield where a goods station was open from 1906 to 1912. Following its closure the line was cut back to the Mill that was served by Gorham's siding where Class J15 No 65447 is seen – no buffer stops were ever erected when the line was truncated, just a pile of sleepers blocked the route towards Halesworth. In later years the mill was used for the storage of potatoes. *Dr Ian C Allen E3092*

Opposite top: In independent days Laxfield was the headquarters of the MSLR, with Superintendent's office and engine shed. No 65447, adorned with a wreath and garland, rolls into the station from Haughley on the last day of service. As is often the case a large number of people turned out, or travelled on the train, to witness the closure of the line. Perhaps if a fraction of those on the platform had travelled, services might have survived until the Beeching era. *Dr Ian C Allen E048*

Opposite bottom: The line's sole locomotive facilities were at Laxfield following closure of Kenton shed in 1912. No 65447 stands alongside the coaling stage, with No 65388 in the somewhat dilapidated building. Following a gale during which the shed lost part of the roof, smoke vents, the doors and end wall, the timber structure was propped up with baulks of timber. Following closure the water tank, seen immediately behind the shed building, was relocated and subsequently sold to the Ffestiniog Railway. *Dr Ian C Allen E3268*

Top: Although initially planned to open with the line, Wilby was a slightly late arrival, opening in July 1909. Facilities were sparse with a corrugated iron hut acting as a booking office and staff room; the GER box wagon body acted as a store. No 65447 arrives from Haughley with three carriages, an open wagon and brake van in tow a few weeks before closure. *Dr Ian C Allen E054*

Bottom: Following closure there is usually a requirement to retrieve any rolling stock remaining on the line. No 65388 is seen with a selection of empty open wagons at Stradbroke ten days after closure. The crew have been joined on the footplate by an official, no doubt to supervise the clearance of items of value. Built in September 1890 as GER No 883, the locomotive was withdrawn in May 1959. *Dr Ian C Allen E037*

The 11.08 Haughley-Laxfield mixed train, behind No 65447, enters Kenton station while the Laxfield-Haughley goods service with No 65361 in charge waits in the loop during 1951. The carriage behind No 65447 – E62334 – was built by the GER (No 947) as a six-wheel three-compartment Brake Third in December 1901; it survived on the MSLR until August 1951 when it was withdrawn. The building in the background is the premises of the East Anglian Farmers Co-operative Ltd, and served by a private siding. No 65361 entered traffic in July 1898; surviving until withdrawal in September 1962, it was one of the last five in service to be withdrawn this month. *Dr Ian C Allen E012*

No 65459 approaches Kenton station, a mile north of the hamlet it was named after, past the down home signal with a mixed train from Haughley. The lower quadrant signal was supplied by Mackenzie & Holland (M&H), who in 1899 in conjunction with the Westinghouse Brake Co was the first to introduce power signalling into Great Britain with an installation at the GER's Bishopsgate station. M&H was formed late in the 19th century and ultimately became part of the Westinghouse Brake Co in 1920. The Class J15 was built in July 1906 and withdrawn in February 1960. This station had been intended to be the junction for the proposed branch to Westerfield, but this line was only two miles (3.2km) in length before construction ceased on the outskirts of Debenham. *Dr Ian C Allen E056*

Top: Early in the summer of 1953 BR issued tenders for the demolition of the line; a firm from Coatbridge in Scotland was awarded the contract. Work commenced in August with BR supplying a train of empty engineers' wagons hauled by No 65404; it is seen here near Brockford & Wetheringsett. Over 100 tons of material were taken away each week with Nos 65388 and 65404 regularly employed removing full wagons before returning with the empties. No 65404 left the Works in November 1891 and was withdrawn at the end of the summer season in October 1956. *Dr Ian C Allen E3240*

Bottom: We return to the main line at Haughley Junction. For what, to many readers, maybe an 'A4' Pacific is actually a streamlined 4-6-0, in this case a Class B17/5. Built as a conventionally-styled Class B17/4 locomotive by Robert Stephenson & Hawthorn in May 1937, it was modified a few months later to the form seen here. One of two, LNER Nos 2858 and 2870 (later BR Nos 61659 and 61670), they were to operate the streamlined 'East Anglian' service between London and Norwich introduced on 27th September 1937, soon after the 'Coronation' and the 'West Riding Limited', but differed from those – and from the 'Silver Jubilee' of 1935 – in several respects in that although new carriages were built, these were neither articulated nor streamlined and there was no special livery. The train ran at speeds not much greater than those achieved by existing expresses on the Norwich line and there was no supplementary fare. No 61670 *City of London* heads south towards Haughley Junction early in the BR era as the tender carries the new owner's title. Both locomotives were rebuilt to conventional form in April 1951 as Class B17/6, with No 61670 surviving in service until April 1960. *Dr Ian C Allen E2799*

Top: When the six-wheeled stock in service on the MSLR was withdrawn in the early 1950s replacement came in the shape of GER bogie coaches dating from the early 1920s, having been built by the Midland Railway Carriage & Wagon Co. Brake Third No E62181 is heading the consist, arriving at Haughley behind Class J15 No 65447; there was obviously no freight traffic on this occasion as the goods brake van has been detached, and left, on the running line to be shunted out of the way before the next service to Laxfield. *Dr Ian C Allen E039*

Bottom: A passenger service prepares to leave Haughley MSLR platform for Laxfield, prior to the station being 'rationalised' by the LNER in 1932/33 to reduce operational costs. Class J65 No 7247 was one of three allocated to work the MSLR in 1926 following its acquisition by the LNER. Classified by the GER as 'E22' these were the smallest of the GER 0-6-0Ts, emerging from Stratford between 1889-1893, with No 7247 entering traffic in February 1893. The 20 class members entered LNER stock, but only four survived until Nationalisation; with No 7247 being withdrawn in February 1948 it never carried its allocated number – 68213. *Dr Ian C Allen E412*

Top: Built at Darlington Works in June 1929 Class J39 No 64787 heads a lengthy freight train north through Haughley station, probably from the docks at Parkestone where it was allocated between June 1951 and March 1958. The 'J39' class consisted of 289 locomotives built between 1926 and 1941 and could be found all over the LNER system working on goods and general mixed traffic duties. The engineers' wagons in front of the grain store and silo appear to be carrying rail and chairs, dating the image to the 1953/4 period when the MSLR was being dismantled.
Dr Ian C Allen E2796

Class B17/6 No 61602 *Walsingham* runs into Haughley with a northbound freight service consisting of 'express' stock, the first two vehicles are Full Brakes, and the following wagon appears to be a milk tanker. Built by the NBL in November 1928, No 61602 was named after a village in north Norfolk famous for its honouring of the Virgin Mary. Walsingham also contains the ruins of two medieval monastic houses and is a centre of pilgrimage. In 1061, according to the legend, an Anglo-Saxon noblewoman, Richeldis de Faverches, had a vision of the Virgin Mary in which she was instructed to build a replica of the house of the Holy Family in Nazareth in honour of the Annunciation. When it was built, the Holy House in Walsingham was panelled with wood and contained a wooden statue of an enthroned Virgin Mary with the child Jesus seated on her lap. No 61602 was built as LNER No 2802, with rebuilding to the form seen here in August 1951. Withdrawal from Yarmouth South Town came in January 1958.
Dr Ian C Allen E3045

Top: In May 1951 three Bulleid Pacifics were transferred from the Southern Region to Stratford Depot – No 34039 *Boscastle* arrived on the 8th, with Nos 34057 *Biggin Hill* and 34065 *Hurricane* following shortly later. On 16th July 1951 a succession of locomotive problems resulted in No 34039 being commandeered to work the Ipswich-Bury St Edmunds local service. It was the first Pacific of any variety to visit Bury and was too long for the 50ft 4in turntable. It is seen here leaving Haughley Junction on the return journey running tender first. No 34039 returned to the Southern in May 1952, Nos 34057 and 34065 returning in May 1952. The speed limit through the main platform is 65mph, with access to the loop platform at 40. *Dr Ian C Allen S48*

Bottom: Class B17/6 No 61634 *Hinchingbrooke* heads a stopping service south from Haughley. Constructed at Darlington Works in June 1931, it was rebuilt to the form seen here in January 1957 but only survived until August 1958 when it was withdrawn from March depot. It was named after Hinchingbrooke House in Huntingdon, Cambridgeshire, which in 1970 became part of Hinchingbrooke School, housing the 6th form. The school was formerly Huntingdon Grammar School that, on the site of what is now the Cromwell Museum in Huntingdon, was attended by Oliver Cromwell and Samuel Pepys. *Dr Ian C Allen E3270*

Top: The station at Stowmarket was opened by the Ipswich & Bury Railway on 24th December 1846. The buildings were Grade II listed in 1972, and restored in 1987. It is reported that some shunting at Stowmarket was carried out by horses as late as 1958. Goods traffic lasted until the mid-1970s, the yard being shunted by a Norwich-based Class 03 diesel shunter until January 1977. Some ICI traffic lasted a few years longer. There was also a very short-lived milk service that ran in the summer of 1981 that originated at Chard Junction in Somerset. Dating from December 1890 as a GER Class R24 (Class J67/1), No 68518 is shunting the yard at Stowmarket. Allocated to Ipswich at Nationalisation, it was withdrawn from there a little over 10 years later. There was a stabling point at Stowmarket consisting of a pit and coal stage; opening in 1920 it enabled a locomotive to stay away from its home shed for an extended period. Closed to steam in 1960, it became a diesel stabling point. *Dr Ian C Allen E880*

Middle: BR Class 7MT No 70012 *John of Gaunt* heads the 1.30pm Liverpool-Norwich express service through Stowmarket. Built at Crewe in May 1951 No 70012 was allocated to Norwich Thorpe from new until reallocated to Stratford in November 1958 – although its duties would have remained much as before. Alongside, Class D16/3 No 62605, a product from Stratford Works in May 1911, waits in the sidings with the carriage stock for a connecting service to Bury St Edmunds. No 62605 was rebuilt with a round top boiler in March 1940, retaining its Victorian-style running boards, and was shedded at Cambridge between December 1955 and withdrawal in June 1957. *Dr Ian C Allen E1488*

Bottom: Class K3/2 No 61820 was constructed at Darlington Works in October 1924 and is seen at the head of an express freight service near Needham Market. The attachment of a box van immediately behind the locomotive may have been to add extra braking power as the open wagons would only have hand brakes. At the time the illustration was taken No 61820 was allocated to Parkeston Quay, arriving there in April 1958 and departing in November 1959. *Dr Ian C Allen E2463*

Linesiding near Barham

Built by the NBL in December 1928 No 2807 *Blickling* is seen at the head of a Cambridge-Ipswich stopping service near Barham. Blickling Hall is a stately home on the Blickling Estate to the north of Aylsham. It was built by the surveyor Robert Lyminge for Sir Henry Hobart between 1616 and 1626, on the site of a late medieval moated hall which it largely replaced. It was supplied with elaborate gardens and a banqueting house, set within two deer parks. In 1940 Lord Lothian bequeathed Blicking to the National Trust, in whose ownership it remains. *Dr Ian C Allen E344*

Class J20 No 8289 started life as GER Class D81 No 1289 in December 1922. The 25 members of the class were the most powerful 0-6-0 locomotives to be built until the Southern Railway's Class Q1 class took to the rails in 1942. No 8289 was renumbered as 4694 under the LNER's 1946 renumbering scheme, and rebuilt as a Class J20/1 in September 1947 when it received a round top boiler identical to those carried by Class B12/3. Withdrawal, as BR No 64694, came at Stratford Depot in May 1955. *Dr Ian C Allen E605*

12

Beccles to Ipswich

Top: The East Suffolk Railway opened in 1854, operating as far as Halesworth, and the line was then extended to Ipswich and Yarmouth South Town in 1859. The Beccles to Lowestoft line opened in the same year. The Waveney Valley line from Tivetshall on the Great Eastern main line reached Beccles in 1863, making the town an important junction on the expanding GER network. Having been at the head of an express service from Liverpool Street, the train has been split in the platform at Beccles with the three leading coaches to be taken on to Lowestoft by the train locomotive, BR Class 7MT No 70000 *Britannia*. The vents have been removed from the roof of the former engine shed (see below); the fireman takes the opportunity to take a breather as the route is comparatively easy for the remainder of the journey. *Dr Ian C Allen BR290*

Seen departing from Beccles with the Yarmouth portion of an express from Liverpool Street is No 67387. Built by the Great Northern Railway at Doncaster Works in December 1903 as No 1537, it was renumbered as 7387 in June 1946, and in January 1952, as BR No 67387, and was assigned to Yarmouth South Town to work push-pull duties to Beccles. The GNR built 60 of what became Class C12, with 49 surviving to be taken into BR stock in 1948, the last example was withdrawn in 1958. No 67387 was taken out of traffic in February 1955 from Yarmouth South Town. *Dr Ian C Allen E3036*

Above: With at least seven carriages in tow Nos 65471 and 62789 double head a Waveney Valley line-Yarmouth South Town Sunday excursion away from Beccles past the former engine shed; closed in 1944 it was given over to private use. Class E4 No 62789 has had a 'back cab' fitted to its tender – making life a little easier for the crew who would have spent half their shift running in reverse – this was removed when the locomotive was reallocated to Cambridge in August 1956. Both locomotives were shedded at Norwich Thorpe for much of their BR career; the crews of both locomotives have spotted ICA by the lineside, suggesting that the shot was pre-arranged. No 62789 was outshopped in July 1896, serving the GER and its successors until December 1957. *Dr Ian C Allen E726*

Right: An express bound for London, Class B17/6 Nos 61656 *Leeds United* and 61664 *Liverpool* double head up Beccles bank on Sunday 4th January 1959. On the down, northbound, line a red flag indicates the line is closed for a maintenance team to work safely. A British Railways lorry is almost camouflaged to the left of the crossing, under the last carriage, with a member of staff watching progress of the train. *Dr Ian C Allen E855*

Opposite top: Class F5 No 67201 was constructed in November 1904 as GER No 788, one of 160 locomotives built to the design. The class was heavy on fuel, giving rise to the nickname of 'gobblers'. It is seen arriving at Beccles with a service off the Waveney Valley line from Tivetshall. The leading carriage is a GER clerestory-fitted bogie coach having two First Class and four Third Class compartments, being designated as a Luggage Composite; they were built from 1900 with the last examples withdrawn in November 1953. Allocated to Lowestoft, No 67201 was withdrawn from there in December 1956. *Dr Ian C Allen E1571*

Opposite bottom: Class F5 2-4-2T No 67199 was one of seven members of the class that were fitted with steam brakes and vacuum-operated push-pull equipment in 1949; the latter can be seen to to the side of the smokebox. No 67199 was allocated to Lowestoft between July and October 1955, and is in the platform at Beccles during this period, viewed from the overbridge that provided public access over the railway. After serving the GER and its successors for over 50 years it was withdrawn from Stratford in February 1957. In the 1950s and 1960s closure and rationalisations saw the remaining line singled, with Beccles reduced to one platform. Decades later, in 2012 a passing loop and additional platform were completed to enable passenger services to be increased. *Dr Ian C Allen E1624*

This page, top: In its 'B17/6' guise, No 61659 *East Anglian* has suffered a decline in both appearance and duties since we saw it earlier in the book as it heads north past the signal box at Brampton. To the east of the station is Brampton Hall, a listed country house built in 1794 of red brick for the Leman family who had long associations in the area. The previous Brampton Hall burned down in 1733. A 16th century farmhouse was built on the same site, known as Brampton Old Hall. Today, both buildings are Grade II listed. The left and centre chimneys above the locomotive boiler were once part of what was the Railway Tavern public house that was alongside the line. *Dr Ian C Allen E970*

This page, bottom: Looking north towards the station at Brampton, where it crosses Station Road, the signal box hides the station building with just the waiting shelter on the Down platform being visible. The Railway Tavern was to the left of the telegraph pole that is holding up one end of someone's washing line. *Dr Ian C Allen E296*

Opposite top: Halesworth station, opened on 4th December 1854, was unusual in that a level crossing was situated across the line so that special 'platforms' had to be swung across the road rather than conventional crossing gates. Although the road has since been closed the 'platforms' can still be seen in situ. On the afternoon of 18th December 1941 a German Dornier bombed the stationhouse, killing the stationmaster, his wife and their young maid. The stationhouse was rebuilt but reduced in size. The Halesworth & District Museum and the offices of Halesworth Area Community Transport now occupy the station building. Double-headed LNER 'B12/3s' head the train; No 61561 leads an unidentified member of the class through Halesworth with a southbound express service for Liverpool Street. By the time the photograph was taken BR Mk 1 coaches were to be seen across the GE lines, and with the exception of the leading carriage the train is composed of the new stock. No 61561 was built in March 1920 and withdrawn in September 1958. The independent 3ft gauge Southwold Railway left Halesworth for the coastal town; opening on 24th September 1879, the line served Wenhaston, Blythburgh and Walberswick. Final passenger trains ran on 11th April 1927, with freight finishing a week later; the final steaming took place on 20th April. Plans are in hand to reopen part of the line and, at the time of writing, a replica of 2-4-0T No 3 *Blyth* is under construction. *Dr Ian C Allen E1948*

Opposite bottom: With two box vans separating the locomotive from the oil tankers, Class K1 No 62035 heads south out of Halesworth. The oil tankers are probably from Anglo-American Oil (a subsidiary of Standard Oil) depot at Oulton Broad, and are carrying ESSO advertising panels attached to the tanks rather than being painted on in the traditional manner. No 62035 was built by NBL in September 1949. Although the locomotive is fitted with electric headlamps, traditional oil lamps had to be carried during daylight hours. Allocated to March depot for much of its career, it was withdrawn from Frodingham in July 1965. *Dr Ian C Allen E1952*

Above: BR Standard Class 7MT No 70002 *Geoffrey Chaucer* leads an express service destined for Liverpool Street through Halesworth while, to the left, Class O1 2-8-0 No 63687 tries to hide in the goods shed before heading south with a freight train. Based on a Robinson design for the Great Central Railway No 63687 started life in February 1918 as part of a series of orders, eventually totalling 521 locomotives, for the Railway Operating Department during World War 1; around half of those built were later taken into capital stock by the LNER. Built as GCR Class 8M by Robert Stephenson & Hawthorns LNER No 6324 avoided conscription during World War 2, although 92 classmates were taken over for war service with many going to Egypt. Rebuilt with a round top boiler to Class O1 in December 1945, No 63687 was allocated to March depot in February 1957 being withdrawn from there in October 1963. No 70002 was delivered new from Crewe Works in March 1951 to Stratford depot, serving on GE lines until November 1963 when it was transferred to the London Midland Region; withdrawal came from Carlisle Kingmoor in January 1967. *Dr Ian C Allen BR156*

Aldeburgh branch

Top: The branch left the main line about half a mile north of Saxmundham station. When the 8½-mile line was first opened, by the ECR, on 12th April 1860 the name of the town was spelt Aldeborough. However, the GER amended the spelling to the more familiar version on 1st June 1875. The fireman of No 65467 checks all is well as the locomotive propels the train clear of the platform in order to run round the train. The Class J15 was built in August 1899 and spent its BR career allocated to Ipswich until withdrawn in April 1959. The locomotive carries its class designation and BR number in full on the buffer beam, in LNER style, with British Railways in full on the tender. *Dr Ian C Allen E4033*

Bottom: With No 65467 running round a passenger service, by now sporting a smokebox number plate, Class J17 No 65513 shunts the yard. Built in November 1900 as a GER Class G58, with a round top boiler, No 65513 was rebuilt with a Belpaire version, as seen here, and classified as a 'J17' in October 1931 – the reversal of the usual LNER practice. Allocated to Ipswich in March 1954, it moved to King's Lynn in April 1960 with withdrawal from Cambridge in March 1961. The building just seen on the right was the engine shed, opening with the line on 12th April 1860, and closing in April 1955 just before DMUs started operating the passenger service. Freight services ceased on 30th November 1959 with closure to passenger traffic on 12th September 1966. *Dr Ian C Allen E1966*

No 65447 is seen again, this time departing Thorpeness station that opened on 29th July 1914, a matter of days before World War 1 was declared. It served a holiday village of the same name that had been developed by G. Stuart Ogilvie, and publicised by John Barrie – the creator of Peter Pan. The passenger facilities were basic with coach bodies supported on concrete blocks. Goods traffic was provided for by a single siding, installed in 1921, to take delivery of, amongst other items, Portland cement for onward delivery to the Thorpeness concrete factory. The station was downgraded to a halt in 1962. The resort failed to develop with the halt serving little more than a nearby golf course. *Dr Ian C Allen E1427*

Right: A change from the usual branch motive power as Class L1 No 67705 is seen at Leiston station with an inspection saloon. The locomotive emerged from Darlington Works in February 1948 carrying number E9004, (the E stood for Eastern, this was before the regional numbering system commenced) it was renumbered as 67705 a couple of months later. Above the locomotive cab can be seen the signal box and to its right the gantry crane at the entrance to the original Richard Garrett & Son's works' private siding. In 1914, following a major fire at the works, it was decided to build a new factory on land that had been owned as a demonstration farm next to the station – accessed from the line leading off to the right. From then on the sites were always known as the 'Old Works' and the 'New Works'. The company joined the Agricultural & General Engineers (AGE) combine in 1919, however it entered receivership in 1932. Later the same year Garretts was purchased by Beyer, Peacock with the business trading as the Richard Garrett Engineering Works until closed in 1981. The line through Leiston still exists as it serves Sizewell nuclear power station, a siding and gantry crane having been constructed about a mile to the east of the former station. Should construction of Sizewell 3 proceed the line should see increased use.
Dr Ian C Allen E1094

73

Class J15 No 65447 is at the head of an Ipswich-Aldeburgh regatta special climbing the 1 in 58 bank away from Saxmundham junction in August 1949. *Dr Ian C Allen E1321*

The Aldeburgh branch left the main line at Saxmundham junction, about half a mile to the north of the station which is where we see Class F6 No 67230 as it crosses the junction on its way to the coast. The 20 locomotives of the class were constructed between April 1911 and January 1912; the locomotive, as GER No 1, was built in October 1911, and was allocated to Ipswich depot between August 1950 and November 1956. Withdrawal came at Stratford in May 1958. *Dr Ian C Allen E2943*

Snape Branch

Today Snape Maltings is an arts complex on the banks of the River Alde. It is best known for its concert hall, which is one of the main sites of the annual Aldeburgh Festival. The Maltings were built in the 1800s by Newson Garrett, a Victorian entrepreneur who purchased the business of Osborne & Fennell, corn and coal merchants of Snape Bridge, in 1841. Within three years of his arrival, Newson Garrett was shipping 17,000 quarters (2 dry pints [1.136 litres]) of barley a year from Snape. Much of this barley would have been destined for breweries, where it had first to be malted. In 1854 he began malting at Snape, and was soon shipping malt, rather than barley, to the breweries. The maltings process at Snape came to an end in the 1960s when Swonnell & Son went into liquidation with seven acres of industrial buildings being left vacant. Thirty acres of land was offered for sale, including dwellings and an inn. George Gooderham, a local farmer and businessman, recognised the potential; purchasing the site he set about finding alternative uses for the buildings. An unidentified 'J15' is shunting the goods yard with Snape Maltings in the background. The yard was somewhat basic without even a locomotive run round loop. The internal sidings of the maltings were far more extensive. Today the maltings are a craft centre and concert hall – any sign on the ground of the railway has long since disappeared. *Dr Ian C Allen E2866*

With the maltings in the background the driver of Class J15 No 65478 looks back watching as the shunter couples the wagons together. Once complete the train will cross the wooden bridge over the River Alde bound for Wickham Market. *Dr Ian C Allen E2562*

Top: Looking in the other direction, Class J15 No 65389 crosses the River Alde heading towards Wickham Market. The bridge was subject to a severe weight restriction that limited the classes of locomotives that were allowed on the branch; however the 'J15s' could run almost anywhere. No 65389, built in October 1890, was in traffic for over 69 years, being withdrawn in April 1960. *Dr Ian C Allen E2591*

Bottom: No 65447 rolls off the Snape branch with a weedkilling train in tow; a thankless task that the railways still have to carry out. Topped and tailed by brake vans – to save shunting movements at the end of various branch lines – the tanks carry water to be mixed with a chemical and then sprayed on to the tracks by the second van towards the end of the rake; on the original image the spray can be seen in action. *Dr Ian C Allen E1042*

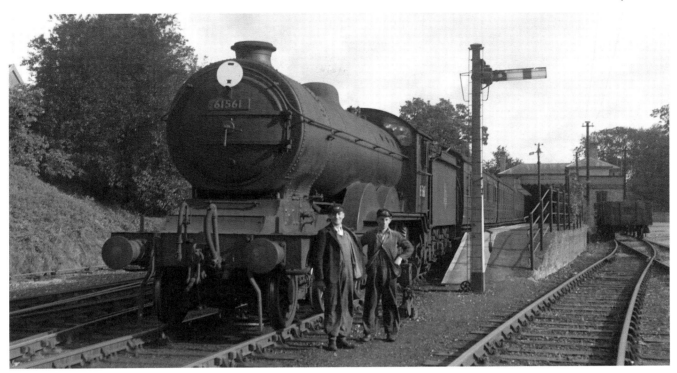

Framlingham Branch

The market town of Framlingham is known for its castle. It started life in the first half of the 12th century as an early motte and bailey or ringwork Norman castle; after a tumultuous history by the end of the 13th century, it had become a luxurious home, surrounded by extensive parkland used for hunting. During the 15th and 16th centuries it was at the heart of the estates of the powerful Mowbray and Howard families. With a large, wealthy household to maintain, the castle purchased supplies from across England and brought in luxury goods from international markets. By the end of the 16th century, however, it fell into disrepair and after the final Howard owner encountered financial difficulties the castle and the surrounding estates were sold off; having a chequered history over the next 400 years. During World War 2, the castle was used by the British military as part of the regional defences against a potential German invasion. Today Framlingham Castle is managed by English Heritage. The branch was opened by the East Suffolk Railway on 1st June 1859 and lost its passenger services on 3rd November 1952, although excursion and college traffic survived for over another decade with the withdrawal of freight services on 19th April 1965. Class B12/3 No 61561's crew pose for the camera with a college special during the goods only era. *Dr Ian C Allen E2499*

Bottom: In the 21st century the town has become well known as the location for Ed Sheeran's song 'Castle on the Hill'. The driver takes the opportunity to pose for ICA's camera as No 65447 engages in shunting carriages from one of the college trains at the terminus. *Dr Ian C Allen E2721*

Top: The halt at Hacheston was an extremely basic affair as this image of it on the Framlingham branch shows. The halt was not opened until 1922 in an attempt by the GER to improve the passenger receipts on the branch; it did not even possess a platform so passengers had to use a ladder to get on and off the trains that called. No 62526 started life in April 1914 as a GER Class S46, No 1875. It was rebuilt by the LNER as a Class D16/3, being renumbered 62526 by BR in 1948. Allocated to Ipswich until June 1953 when it was transferred to March, withdrawal came in May 1957. *Dr Ian C Allen E3342*

Bottom: Class B12/3 No 61564 heads along the Framlingham branch at the head of a beginning of term special in September 1955. The train is made up from a mix of BR and LNER carriage stock, with the third vehicle – a Gresley Vestibule Brake Third – carrying the students' belongings. Framlingham College was founded in 1864 in memory of Queen Victoria's husband, Albert, Prince Consort, whose statue takes pride of place at the front of the College. The Prep School for 3 to 13 year old boys and girls was established in 1948 and officially opened in 1949 in the idyllic neo-Tudor Hall beside the River Deben, approximately five miles from the Senior School in the village of Brandeston. The Hall, known as Brandeston Hall, was bought by the Society of Old Framlinghamians to remember those who fell in the two World Wars. No 61564 was built in April 1920, serving until November 1958. *Dr Ian C Allen E1612*

A very smart Class B1 No 61253 hauls the ex-LMS Royal Train southwards off the Framlingham branch whilst classmate No 61399 waits on the main line to take the train northwards. It was common practice to stable the Royal Train overnight on quiet branch lines – any normal passenger traffic would have been replaced by buses, but as the line was closed to passenger traffic only freight traffic might have been disrupted. Both locomotives were built by the NBL, No 61253 in November 1947, with No 61399 in April 1952; withdrawal came in September 1962 and September 1963 respectively.
Dr Ian C Allen E1737

Class F5 2-4-2T No 7140 takes the branch at Wickham Market junction as it heads its two-coach train to Framlingham. The GER Class M15 was introduced between 1884 and 1909, with withdrawals starting in 1913. No 7140 did not make it into BR ownership.
Dr Ian C Allen E569

Opposite top: Class L1 No 67711 heads a train of milk tankers and bogie vans south past the Framlingham branch junction. As the contents of the tanks would have been perishable the train was 'express' rated with all vehicles being fitted with brakes. No 67711 emerged from Darlington Works in March 1948 as LNER No E9010, before renumbering the following month. It was in traffic for less than 13 years, being withdrawn from Stratford depot in December 1960. *Dr Ian C Allen E1709*

Opposite bottom: Wickham Market station was opened by the East Suffolk Railway on 1st June 1859, the same date as the Framlingham branch; the company was absorbed by the ECR the same day. It was actually located around two miles to the east of the town in Campsea Ashe, the staggered platforms were accessed via a foot crossing as no footbridge was provided. Today the line is singled so cross-platform access is not a problem. Whilst the Framlingham branch retained its freight services until April 1965, Wickham Market lost its on 13th July 1964. Class B17/6 No 61655 *Middlesbrough* is in charge of a northbound express passenger service; built at Darlington Works in April 1936, it spent its BR career allocated to Stratford or Cambridge and was withdrawn in April 1959. *Dr Ian C Allen E1426*

Felixstowe Pier line

Above: The Felixstowe Railway & Pier (FR&P) opened on 1st May 1877 but initially there were no stations between Orwell and the terminus at Felixstowe Pier as the station near the beach at Felixstowe was not ready in time. An additional intermediate station later opened at Trimley on 1st May 1891. The FR&P had been promoted by Colonel George Tomline who owned property in the area. The station at Felixstowe Beach has clearly seen better days as its bay platform road is being used to empty coal wagons. It lost its passenger services on 11th September 1967, with general freight going in December 1966. Dismantling of the infrastructure is under way as there is a pile of 'rodding stools' on the platform. The line remains open for freight trains to Felixstowe Docks. *Dr Ian C Allen MISC147*

At the north end of the Beach station the FR&P built an engine shed; opening the same day as the line, the facilities included a two-road shed, water tank and coal stage. By 1938 the building had become derelict; a servicing point was established with locomotives continuing to make use of the sidings, and facilities until the early BR era. The only identifiable locomotive is LNER No 8841, a Class D16/2; it was renumbered as 2552 in August 1946, and again as 62552 following Nationalisation. *Dr Ian C Allen E449*

Looking towards the buffer stops a brake van occupies the end of the centre road of Felixstowe Town station, which was opened by the GER on 1st July 1898. With general freight traffic ceasing on 5th December 1966 the extensive track layout was retained to handle the increasing dock traffic. Following the opening of a direct link to the docks the layout was rationalised with a short single line platform remaining in use. *Dr Ian C Allen E2973*

Returning to the main line, on 21ˢᵗ July 1845, the Ipswich & Bury St Edmunds Railway had secured the rights to build a line from Ipswich to Woodbridge but construction was delayed for financial reasons. The station at Westerfield, junction for the later Felixstowe line, opened on 1ˢᵗ June 1859. The company was absorbed by the EUR on 9ᵗʰ July 1847, which extended the line to Norwich, opening on 12ᵗʰ December 1849. Class B17/6 No 61656 *Leeds United* heads an express bound for Liverpool Street just to the north of the station. *Dr Ian C Allen E1319*

On 1ˢᵗ June 1859 the main line was opened by the EUR as far south as Westerfield and Ipswich and north to Yarmouth Southtown; in 1862 the GER took over operation of the line. The Felixstowe branch line opened in 1877. In 1885 an ambitious Midland Railway scheme would, had it come to fruition, have seen Westerfield junction linked to Chesterton junction just north of Cambridge. Like so many schemes of the time it foundered and died a natural death. Class J15 No 65389 is taking the main line through the station with a short train of open wagons. Built as GER Class Y14 No 886 in October 1890, the locomotive remained in service until April 1960 when it was withdrawn from Parkeston Quay depot. *Dr Ian C Allen E1801*

13

Norwich Thorpe to Ely

Top: The Trowse Swing Bridge, originally built in 1845 by George Parker Bidder, was rebuilt in 1905 and again in 1987. The 1905 bridge is seen here with a single red flag flying indicating that the bridge is operational. The carriage sidings to the right of the swing bridge are today part of Norwich Crown Point depot, while the factory on the left was the Gothic Electrical Engineering Works. The current single-track rail bridge on the electrified railway line in to Norwich was designed by BR Eastern Region engineers based in York. The main contractor was May Gurney of Norwich and they were also the civil works contractor. The Butterley Engineering Co (BEC) was the fabricators, mechanical contractor and electrical contractor. The bridge was fabricated and fully trial erected, including a slewing motion trial, inside the BEC's workshops known as 'The Bridge Yard' at Butterley Hill, Ripley, in Derbyshire, during 1986 and was delivered to site and installed during the winter months of November 1986 to January 1987. Like many swing bridges, the structure first lifts on hydraulic jacks before swinging open to allow the passage of water traffic. It is notable for being the only one in the United Kingdom to carry an overhead electrified railway track with power supply to trains provided by an overhead conductor rail instead of a wire; there are short lengths of overhead conductor rail either side of the bridge on the fixed approaches. There is a 40mph (64km/h) speed limit over the bridge in both directions as trains are about to arrive at, or have just departed from, Norwich station. *Dr Ian C Allen MISC052*

Bottom: Stanier LMS Class 8F 2-8-0 No 48750, heading the last scheduled steam-hauled freight train to Norwich, is seen passing through the closed Trowse station on 12th December 1963. Located very close to Norwich it was closed as a cost cutting measure during World War 1 between 22nd May 1916 and 31st March 1919 and again from 5th September 1939. It was re-opened briefly in March 1986 when Norwich was closed for electrification works and it served as the line's northern terminus for all of three days. No 48750 was built by the LNER at Darlington Works in August 1946, as its Class O6 and numbered 3145, renumbered as 3545 in April 1947 before it was loaned to the LMS in October 1947 to become No 8750 in their '8F' number series. *Dr Ian C Allen M426*

Top: Some youngsters enjoy the view of two BR Class 7MT 'Britannias' at Trowse Upper junction, this was where the lines into Norwich Victoria and Thorpe split. No 70001 *Lord Hurcomb* is at the head of the Down (London Liverpool Street-Norwich Thorpe) 'Norfolkman' service. Meanwhile No 70013 *Oliver Cromwell* has just reversed up the bank from Trowse Lower junction with a Whitemoor-Norwich freight service – this move was necessary as there was no direct connection into Victoria, from the Wymondham direction; Class J69 0-6-0T No 68555 was attached to the other end for the movement. The Eastern Union Railway's Norwich Victoria station had closed to passenger services in 1916, but remained in use as a general goods depot until 1966. *Dr Ian C Allen BR48*

Bottom: Running towards Norwich off the Ipswich line at the head of a freight service, Class K3/2 No 61953 stands in the loop alongside an unidentified classmate at Trowse Lower junction. No 61953 was built by the NBL in October 1935 and spent three periods of its BR career allocated to Norwich Thorpe – October 1947-August 1948, December 1948-October 1953 and January 1954-December 1960 – the in between time was spent at Lowestoft shed. Allocated away from the GE in December 1960 it was withdrawn from Doncaster depot in October 1961. The lines to the left take services west via Wymondham and Thetford to Ely by passing under the Ipswich line a couple of miles away. *Dr Ian C Allen E3956*

The Bill for the Norwich & Brandon Railway (N&BR) received Royal Assent on 10th May 1844. Work started on the line in 1844 and, with its stations, was opened on 30th July 1845. The line ran from Ely to Trowse, in Norwich. The final link into Norwich (Thorpe) was delayed due to the need to build a bridge over the River Wensum that kept the river navigable. On 15th February 1847 Wymondham became a junction with the opening of the line to Wells via Dereham. An unidentified Class J17 is making up its freight train at Wymondham before departing in the Norwich direction. Up until 2009 there was a telegraph pole route in operation between Wymondham and Brandon. This was removed gradually during the early part of 2009 and was the last section remaining in England and one of the last remaining in the United Kingdom. In 2012 the local signal box was closed and the semaphore signalling was replaced by lightweight LED signals controlled from Cambridge. *Dr Ian C Allen E4067*

Class J15 No 65471 entered service in June 1913 as GER No 543, receiving its BR number in November 1949 almost two years after Nationalisation; it spent its BR career allocated to Norwich Thorpe depot. It is seen taking the Wells line at the junction immediately to the south of Wymondham station with an empty milk train consisting of a full brake and single tanker bound for North Elmham. Today this is the junction of the Mid-Norfolk Railway, a heritage route to Dereham, although those services operate from a separate station named Wymondham Abbey which is approximately one mile from the main line station and, as the name suggests, is near to the abbey. *Dr Ian C Allen E2190*

Top: 'Britannia' Class 7MT No 70003 *John Bunyan* passes over the level crossing at Spooner Row at the head of an express service to Norwich. The station was opened on 30th July 1845 by the N&BR who closed it in September 1847. In 1848 the N&BR was absorbed by the Eastern Counties Railway who reopened the station on 1st December 1855. The station closed for a second time on 1st August 1860. An Act of Parliament on 7th August 1862 authorised the amalgamation of the ECR and the Eastern Union Railway, which resulted in the formation of the GER. Subsequent to this, Spooner Row was opened for the third time on 1st March 1882. Freight services ceased on 13th July 1964. Today, it is one of the least-used passenger stations in Norfolk, with just 1,344 entries/exits in 2018/19, according to Office of Rail & Road estimates, though this figure was a marked increase on just 264 six years prior. There is a very limited passenger service to Cambridge and Norwich. Built at Crewe in March 1951, No 70003 was later transferred to the London Midland Region and withdrawn in March 1967. *Dr Ian C Allen BR257*

Bottom: Passing Thetford West junction the school train from Swaffham, via Watton, is in the control of double-headed Class D16/3s, with No 62601 acting as pilot engine. The junction served as the northern end of the line south to Bury St Edmunds. No 62601 entered traffic in February 1911 as GER No 1790; rebuilt as a 'D16/3' in September 1944 its first BR depot was Cambridge before reallocation to King's Lynn. Five years after Nationalisation BR decided to close the Thetford to Bury St Edmunds line to passenger services. Thetford lost its status as a passenger junction on 8th June 1953; freight traffic continued until 27th June 1960. *Dr Ian C Allen E1368*

This page, top: The southern end of the service via Holme Hale to Swaffham was Thetford where Class D16/3 No 62564 and Class C12 No 67360 are seen heading west towards Roudham Junction with the double-headed schools service. The station has received a Grade II listing as being of historic importance as 'an early example of a station building by an independent railway company during the heroic age of railway expansion'. No 62564 entered traffic as a GER Class S46, No 1833, in April 1904; being rebuilt as a 'D16/3' in January 1948 it was withdrawn from Lincoln depot in March 1958. *Dr Ian C Allen E1021*

This page, bottom; Class F6 No 67238 rolls into Thetford station past the signal box at the head of a two-coach stopping passenger service. Built as GER Class G69, No 9, in January 1912 it survived until November 1955. The signal box was decommissioned in June 2012 and although derelict is listed as part of the station environs. A holiday destination, for those without private road transport, Thetford is the nearest station to the Center Parcs holiday village at Elveden Forest, approximately five miles to the west. *Dr Ian C Allen E2432*

Opposite top: The railway between Bury St Edmunds and Thetford was proposed by the Bury St Edmunds & Thetford Railway (B&TR) and authorised on 5th July 1865; but the company had problems in raising the necessary money. After assistance was given by the Thetford & Watton Railway (T&WR), the plan was modified, and instead of running to the main station at Thetford, a curve was built so that T&WR trains from Swaffham could run directly to the Bury St Edmunds line without reversing at Thetford. This curve was opened first, on 15th November 1875, along with Thetford Bridge station. The B&TR line between Bury St Edmunds and Thetford Bridge was opened on 1st March 1876. The B&TR was purchased by the GER in 1878. Trains on the B&TR were operated by the T&WR until 1879, when operation was taken over by the GER; after this, trains from Bury began to run to Thetford; the east to south curve at Thetford Bridge was not used after 1880. Thetford Bridge was then the last station before Thetford. The station closed to passenger services on 8th June 1953 with the line closing to freight traffic on 27th June 1960. Class J17 No 65528 entered traffic as GER Class F48 No 1178 in October 1901 and was rebuilt to the form seen here in March 1923. It is seen at the north end of the station with two Gresley-designed horse boxes and brake van in tow; as the locomotive is not fitted with a train brake the boxes would have been empty as loaded ones would need to be hauled by a fitted locomotive to avoid violent movement when braking. *Dr Ian C Allen E2110*

Opposite bottom: The Norwich breakdown train is seen at the southern end of Thetford Bridge behind Class J15 No 65469. As the headlamp displays a 'through mineral or empty wagon train' headcode it is likely to be recovering equipment following closure of the line – particularly as part of the consist has been left beyond the home signal that is in the 'off' position. Generally the crane would not be taken out unless it was required, tool vans carrying items useful for rerailing stock would have been the usual choice. The carriage, No E961521, is branded Motive Power Running Department – Norwich; it started life as a GER Saloon before being transferred to departmental use. *Dr Ian C Allen E2364*

Opposite top: A couple of miles to the south the line ran alongside the one of the RAF Expansion Period Air Ammunition Parks, a siding connected the site to Barnham station. In 1941 the site became a Forward Ammunition Depot resulting in explosives and chemicals being required. With the Depot capable of holding 20,000 tons, the station at Barnham handled 132,729 wagon loads of explosives totalling 721,000 tons during World War 2. There was often a train in the reception sidings, at the station and a third waiting along the line. On one occasion there were 105 wagons at the site with a further 60 waiting at Bury St Edmunds; after the war bombs and chemicals from other sites arrived for disposal with the site closing in 1954. No 65405, a member of the 'J15' class, is seen at Barnham; having been built in November 1891, as GER No 911, it survived in service until August 1958. *Dr Ian C Allen E2480*

Opposite bottom: Class F6 No 67238 is seen at Seven Hills Halt with a Thetford-Bury St Edmunds service; it was shedded at Bury from August 1953 to June 1953. The platform, opened on 20th December 1922, was the length of just a single carriage, alighting passengers had to be careful to avoid a long drop to the ground. The goods yard here is recorded as closing on 1st May 1918, although as can be seen a siding is still in evidence some 45 years later, presumably it remained in situ for agricultural traffic. Final closure to freight was scheduled for 27th June 1960, however, a trip over the line was organised for Saturday 11th June. The special made use of a motley selection of three LMS and two LNER guards vans for the 'passengers', hauled by a remarkably clean 'J15' No 65469. *Dr Ian C Allen E2422*

Above: Returning to the main line, the town of Brandon is situated along the northern boundary of Suffolk with the station actually located in Norfolk, the border sign being immediately south of the level crossing to the west of the station. Class D16/2 No 8851 heads a Liverpool Street-Lowestoft express through open countryside just to the east of the station in July 1936. In 2020, Greater Anglia planned to demolish the historic 1840s station building to enlarge the car park. On 6th May 2020 Greater Anglia confirmed that it had been granted permission to carry out the work which was expected to begin by the end of the year. In spite of objections by the local parish council and others, Breckland District Council said, 'The only issues of consideration ... are the method of demolition and site restoration. The purpose of this application is not to assess the historical merit of the building and potential restoration of the building.' However, according to Historic England, railway stations of such an early date are considered to be 'of international significance as being among the earliest railway structures in the world, and even partial survivals need to be assessed carefully.' Nevertheless, the Railway Heritage Trust (sponsored by Network Rail and Highways England) did not support the objectors' cause. However SAVE arranged for plans to be drawn up for an office conversion, in another attempt to preserve the building. In August 2020 the planned demolition was put on hold following campaign group SAVE Britain's Heritage launching judicial proceedings. At the end of August the station was granted Grade II listed status. *Dr Ian C Allen E430*

14

Haughley to Newmarket

Above: The western end of Bury St Edmunds station with No 67238 taking water. It was allocated to Bury at Nationalisation and again between August 1952 and June 1953. Of note is the 'fire devil', by the water crane, used to keep the liquid flowing during winter weather. Originally suffixed 'Northgate', the station was designed by Sancton Wood (1815-66), built in 1847 replacing a temporary one that opened with the line a short time earlier. The station building is now Grade II listed. *Dr Ian C Allen E1187*

Opposite top: On 21st April 1885 a non-timetabled station called Warren Hill was opened at the north end of Warren Hill Tunnel in Newmarket with the encouragement of the Jockey Club. It was built by the GER to cater for the increasing number of passengers arriving from the east and the north on race days particularly from Lincoln, Leeds and Manchester. There were three parallel sidings on the north side of the platform and two on the south to accommodate waiting excursion trains. Warren Hill remained in use until at least 1945 but had closed by Nationalisation in 1948 (some publications give different opening and closing dates). Class E4 No 62785 heads a two-coach train from Ely past the signal box at Warren Hill on the 'through line' bypassing the now abandoned platforms. Immediately to the north of Warren Hill station was a triangular junction that allowed trains to run either to Ely or Ipswich (or direct between the two locations) – hence the multitude of signals. There were also sidings and a coal depot where the fuel was stored for the Bury St Edmunds locomotive depot. The platform at Warren Hill was also used for loading coal. The Newmarket to Ely line closed to all traffic on 13th September 1965 and with it the Snailwell chord of the three-way junction. *Dr Ian C Allen E991*

Opposite bottom: The main Newmarket station was at the southern end of the 1,000yd (1,006m) Warren Hill Tunnel where No 62785 is seen departing with the return service to Ely. The first railway station in Newmarket opened in 1848 as the terminus of the Newmarket & Chesterford Railway. This station was extended with an island platform and opened along with the Newmarket to Ely line in 1879. The former terminus became known as Newmarket (High Level). The leading carriage is No E18186E; a Gresley Vestibule Composite Corridor dating from 1935 it survived in traffic until November 1961. A lone horsebox can be seen behind the signal post. *Dr Ian C Allen E4091*

15

Bury St Edmunds to Marks Tey

Top: GER Class T26 No 490 entered traffic in January 1895, becoming 62785 at Nationalisation. Allocated to Bury St Edmunds depot in the late 1940s it is seen here passing the site of Bury St Edmunds Eastgate station. Opened with the line, as Eastgate Street, by the GER on 9th May 1865 the station was an early closure with passenger services ceasing on 1st May 1909 – the main line station being more convenient as it connected with services on the Newmarket-Haughley line. Allocated to Bury St Edmunds depot in the late 1940s, No 62785 is seen passing the site of the platform on its way south; despite the fact that the station never handled goods traffic, there was once a siding opposite the southern end of the platform. Although the station closed in 1909, it was used in July 1914 for the Suffolk Agricultural Show. Whilst the track bed here now lies beneath the A14 dual carriageway, No 62785 – withdrawn in December 1959 – survives in preservation at the Bressingham Steam Museum as part of the National Collection. *Dr Ian C Allen E2785*

Bottom: Situated at the end of Station Hill was Welnetham station, which even today is in the middle of nowhere. The station had a single platform on the west side of the line. The main station building was brick built and incorporated a two-storey stationmaster's house with a single storey block attached that included the booking office waiting room with a separate gents' toilet at the north end. The part of the building containing the booking office was slightly recessed with a small canopy between the two projecting ends of the building. There was a small goods yard that consisted of a single siding accessed from either direction; it ran partially behind the platform. The station handled a limited range of goods traffic, but not livestock. A timber goods lock-up was provided on the platform adjacent to the gents' toilet. Access to the yard was controlled by a signal box on the up side of the line opposite the north end of the platform. The guard has given the right of way as Class C12 No 67385 heads southwards. The locomotive was constructed by the GNR at Doncaster in December 1903, and transferred to Bury St Edmunds depot in November 1952 from where it was withdrawn in April 1955. The reason why the station was not situated further north near the village of Sicklesham has probably been lost in the mists of time. *Dr Ian C Allen E3310*

Top: Class F6 No 67237 arrives at Cockfield with the station porter waiting with a couple of packages to be placed in the brake compartment under the care of the guard. Introduced into traffic in December 1912 it was allocated to Bury St Edmunds at Nationalisation, moving briefly to King's Lynn shed and returning in November 1949 for three years with a final stint from June 1953 before withdrawal in August the same year. Opened as Cockfield, the station was renamed Cockfield (Suffolk) on 1st October 1927 to avoid confusion with Cockfield in Durham which was itself renamed Cockfield Fell in 1923. A private siding ran from the goods yard to the adjacent Cockfield Hall. The hall, which was demolished in 1888, was bought by the renowned Newmarket trainer Thomas Jennings in 1865 and turned into a stud farm. He built the southern block of the buildings for use as mares' boxes with an exercise yard, and the eastern strip as a cart lodge with a granary over it. When the railway arrived in 1870 a siding was provided terminating under it so that grain sacks could be lowered into wagons. The siding was also used for bringing in cattle from Wales and animal feed in the form of sugar beet pulp from Bury St Edmunds. The siding was taken out of use c1940 when a tank trap was dug all the way along the western side of the line as part of the wartime defences. These were backed up with the row of pillboxes manned by the Home Guard. The station closed to passenger traffic on 10th April 1961, with final closure to goods traffic between Bury and Lavenham on 19th April 1965. *Dr Ian C Allen E2714*

Bottom: Lavenham with Class E4 No 62797 heading away with the local service to Bury St Edmunds. The train is made up from an Articulated Twin set (two carriages running on a common centre bogie), these sets were generally used on suburban services. To a Gresley-design, the set seen here, consisting of a Brake Third and Composite (1st/3rd class), has been cascaded from the Nottingham and West Riding area. In the goods yard Class J19 No 64659, built in January 1917 as GER Class T77 No 1149, pauses whilst making up its train which seems to consist mainly of empty wagons. *Dr Ian C Allen E1662*

With track lifting in place between Long Melford and Lavenham, No 61287 provides the motive power as the 'wrecking crew' seems more interested in chatting – perhaps something has broken! The 'B1' was built by NBL in February 1948; allocated to Cambridge when new it moved to March depot in June 1962 from where it was withdrawn in September the same year. *Dr Ian C Allen E2394*

To the north of Long Melford station was the junction where the line from Cambridge via Haverhill connected with the Marks Tey-Bury St Edmunds line. Cross-country routes were often used for long distance services to holiday destinations so as to avoid conjestion on main lines and the need to reverse direction of travel. Most of the junctions to east coast destinations faced London. Travelling from the northwest this route enabled direct links to the Clacton, Harwich and Felixstowe lines.
The driver of Class B17/6 No 61623 *Lambton Castle* has the single line token in hand as the train approaches the signal box at Long Melford. The locomotive emerged from Darlington Works in February 1931 as a 'B16/2', it was rebuilt to the form seen here in April 1948 and spent its BR career allocated to Cambridge with withdrawal coming in July 1959. The locomotive was named for Lambton Castle that stands above Chester-le-Street, Co Durham; it is the ancestral seat of the Lambton family, the Earls of Durham. In 2012, the Grade II* listed castle was the setting of the television drama 'The Paradise'. *Dr Ian C Allen E795*

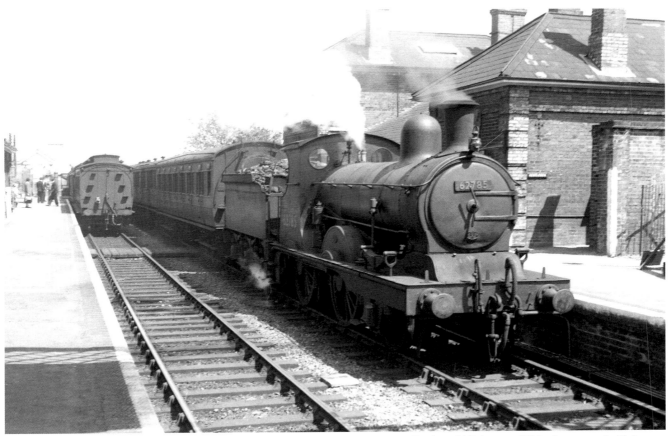

Top: Opened on 9th August 1865 as Melford the station was renamed as Long Melford on 1st February 1884, at a somewhat later date Class E4 No 62785 heads a Marks Tey service. The last carriage in the Bury service is a clerestory Third, that must be one of the last in BR service; three carriages were modified for use on Conductor Train Services enabling station booking offices to be closed as a method of cost saving. A proposal to extend services by building a light railway between here and Hadleigh was reported in the *Haverhill Echo* on 10th March 1900. A Light Railway Order was granted on 8th February 1901 for the Long Melford & Hadleigh Light Railway, however, no construction work was carried out and the line was never built. *Dr Ian C Allen E527*

Bottom: With an air of dereliction already surrounding the goods yard at Long Melford, there was little in the way of freight although the coal merchant, on the extreme right of the image, may still be making use of rail transport – closure to general goods was with effect from 6th April 1964. Class D16/3 No 62558 heads a Colchester service away from the station whilst the northbound train (just visible through the footbridge) departs. Built in December 1906, as GER No 1847, it was rebuilt in September 1948 – retaining the decorative valance over the driving wheels – and as No 62558 saw service until withdrawn in May 1957.
Dr Ian C Allen E4203

The first Sudbury station was built by the Colchester, Stour Valley, Sudbury & Halstead Railway; even before opening on 30th July 1849 the line had been leased by the Ipswich & Bury Railway who in turn merged with the EUR in early 1849. The initial station was a single platformed terminus station at the end of a single-track line from Marks Tey, from where services shared tracks with the ECR into Colchester. The original station was replaced in 1865 by the GER when the line was extended to Cambridge to create the Stour Valley Railway. The station was unstaffed from 14th August 1966 when Paytrain operation of the line commenced with general goods services withdrawn on 31st October 1966. Sudbury became a terminus again following the rationalisation of railway services that included the closure of the Stour Valley line as a through route on 6th March 1967. Trains are crossing with Class J15 No 65461 in charge of the Marks Tey/Colchester service. No 65461 entered traffic in February 1912, serving until April 1960. The current, 1990-built, station is roughly on the site of the loading dock occupied by the horse boxes to the right of the image.
Dr Ian C Allen E681

The shunter looks towards the camera, with shunting pole in hand, as Class J20 No 64696 pauses whilst shunting the yard. Built in December 1922, as GER Class D81 No 1291, it lasted in service until April 1962 being withdrawn from March depot. In the background is the former St Peters Church; now a cultural venue the building is recorded in the National Heritage List for England as a designated Grade I listed building, and is under the care of the Churches Conservation Trust. A church has been on the site since at least 1180, but the current structure dates from the 15th century, though there have been several restorations in the intervening period. The stonework of the exterior was restored in 1911, when statues were inserted into three niches in the south porch. A further restoration took place in 1968 when the upper part of the tower was replaced and the spire was taken down. The church was declared redundant in 1972. The engine shed covered the middle siding to the right of the image. *Dr Ian C Allen E1442*

Pausing between duties is Class J15 No 65475, GER Class Y14 No 547. The locomotive pit is all that remains of the shed that was tucked away in the goods yard when the original station was abandoned. The building was demolished during the early BR period, remaining as a stabling and servicing point for steam until final closure in October 1959 – No 65475 was withdrawn that September. Diesel multiple-units were introduced on 1st January 1959 and they continued to use the siding for stabling. The cattle vans on the left occupy the original platform line now being used as a cattle dock. Note the rudimentary workbench with vice and two fire buckets. *Dr Ian C Allen E2458*

In 1889 extensive resignalling took place, with block working introduced on the line through Sudbury. In addition to the existing signal box located just west of Sudbury station, Sudbury Goods Junction signal box was commissioned, located east of the station it controlled the level crossing and entrance to the goods yard and locomotive shed. During the depression of the 1930s the LNER introduced economies with the closure of the station signal box, with all signalling transferred to the Sudbury Goods Junction box. This was retained to operate the level crossing following dieselisation despite the fact that all of the track except the platform line was removed; closure of the box came on 15th February 1981. Class B1 No 61066 runs into the station tender first with a train consisting of mainly loaded open wagons; built by NBL in August 1946, it was withdrawn in September 1962. *Dr Ian C Allen E3625*

Top: Class B17/6 No 61666 *Nottingham Forest* leads a Colchester-Cambridge service into Sudbury past an unidentified Class J17 waiting in the siding with a goods train. Built by Robert Stephenson & Hawthorn in February 1937, No 61666 entered traffic as a Class B17/4 numbered 2866, it was rebuilt with a round top boiler in December 1947 and withdrawn from Stratford depot in March 1960. A siding, leading off to the right,used to connect to a dock alongside the River Stour.
Dr Ian C Allen E3287

Bottom: A case of overkill as Class B17/6 No 61642 *Kilverstone Hall* approaches Bures with an Articulated Twin set in tow. The station opened with the line and having escaped Dr Beeching's attentions remains open, albeit unstaffed. On 12th July 1887 one person was killed at Bures when part of a runaway train collided with a crossing gate.
Dr Ian C Allen E2652

Top: Although originating from the LMS a batch of Ivatt-designed Class 2MTs were allocated to GE metals from new. No 46466 was built at the former LNER Darlington Works in June 1951 and initially allocated to Cambridge depot; it was transferred to March shed in June 1962 only to be withdrawn two months later. It is seen here heading towards Marks Tey with a Cambridge-Colchester service.
Dr Ian C Allen M530

Bottom: Heading north Class E4 No 62792 enters Chappel & Wakes Colne station. It opened with the line on 2nd July 1849 as Chappel and was renamed Chappel & Wakes Colne on 1st October 1914. The goods yard is now the location of the East Anglian Railway Museum; the platform buildings, on the station's west side, restored to 1950s style, are part of the museum, and entered from ground-floor level. Sitting just to the south of the station is the outstanding feature on the line, the 1,066ft (325m) long viaduct consisting of 32 arches each having a 30ft (9.15m) span and standing 75ft (22.86m) above the valley floor. Built at a cost of £32,000 it contains seven million bricks, with the vast majority manufactured on-site using local clay.
Dr Ian C Allen E1769

Ipswich to Colchester

Top: The EUR opened its first terminus in Ipswich – called Ipswich Stoke Hill – in 1846 on Station Road at the southern end of the tunnel, close to the old quay for the steamboats and the aptly named Steamboat Tavern. The Ipswich Steam Navigation Co had been formed in 1824/25 during a period of steamship mania and briefly offered services from the quay between Ipswich and London calling at Walton-on-the-Naze. The current station is just to the north of Stoke tunnel, which was constructed as part of the Ipswich to Ely line opening as far as Bury St Edmunds in late 1846. The station was re-sited to its present location in 1860 and when the new station was completed, a new road (Princes Street) linking the station to the town was also opened. As built, the station had a single main through platform with some shorter ay platforms at the north end. The island platform at Ipswich was added by the GER in 1883. Built as a GER Class S69 No 1510 in April 1913, and renumbered 8510 in January 1924, it is seen awaiting departure with an express passenger service from Liverpool Street. Allocated BR No 61510, it spent its short BR career at Stratford depot; withdrawal came in June 1949, without it being renumbered. *Dr Ian C Allen E628*

Bottom: Locomotive activity started on the depot site with the opening of the original Ipswich station located at Croft Street and (presumably the newly named) Station Street in June 1846 by the EUR.

Locomotives belonging to sister company, the Ipswich & Bury Railway, would also have used the facilities when their line opened in November 1846 although the two railway companies were worked as one from January the following year. In 1854 the EUR was taken over by the ECR and in 1860 the new station opened after the tunnel was completed. It was at this time that a carriage and wagon works was established on the site of the old station. The initial engine shed was a two-road shed with associated sidings and a small (befitting the size of engine of the time) turntable. The history of the shed for the next 90 or so years was a case of poor facilities being provided for what was a busy depot, and head of a significantly sized organisational district including major sub-sheds at Colchester and Parkeston as well as a host of smaller sheds. During World War 2 a US Army Class S160 2-8-0 was allocated to the shed for a few weeks in 1943; some of the class were allocated to Stratford and March that would have visited Ipswich during this time. The depot was completely rebuilt in 1954 into a concrete six track straight through road shed. The shed building at Ipswich was rebuilt in 1954. Other major improvements included the installation of a mechanical coaling plant and covered inspection pit. Designed to facilitate dieselisation, the depot closed to steam on 2nd November 1958 and diesels 10 years later. The 20 members of Class J65 were built in 1889-1893 being the smallest variety of 0-6-0Ts built by the GER as its Class E22, only four entered service with BR and just two were renumbered, with No 68211 surviving in traffic until November 1953; it is seen here, possibly stored as its leading coupling rods have been removed. *Dr Ian C Allen E1727*

Top: Class B1 No 61058 was built by NBL in July 1946 and was allocated to Ipswich until November 1959, when it moved to Immingham. It is seen here on shed having been spruced up by the cleaners, complete with white-washed guard irons, buffers and smokebox door fittings; no doubt that it was for a special working of some nature as fireman Robertson (left), foreman Bill Thurlow, shop officemen Claud Sanson and Percy Coates pose alongside for their picture to be taken. *Dr Ian C Allen E701*

Bottom: A trio of 'B12/3s' – Nos 61566, 61561 and 61570 – are on shed at Ipswich prior to working afternoon trains to London; they would have been serviced on arrival, being turned with tenders coaled and watered. ICA is standing looking over one of the stacking areas that were used for storing coal that would have been purchased at 'summer' prices to await the forthcoming winter. *Dr Ian C Allen E1136*

Two Class J70 tram locomotives are seen on shed; 12 were built by the GER between 1903 and 1921 for use on the Wisbech & Upwell tramway, Yarmouth and Ipswich docks. The dock locomotives were only fitted with 'cow-catchers', as seen here, the W&U ones had side shields as well to cover the wheels and motion. No 68216 entered traffic in October 1903, as GER No 135, withdrawal came in November 1953; No 68220 was a later example, commencing service as GER No 130 in April 1910 serving until February 1952. The class was extinct by August 1955. *Dr Ian C Allen E2811*

Ipswich shed on a Sunday morning in May 1952 with Class J17 No 65510 shunting the yard in preparation for Monday's commuter services – it was always useful to have the locomotives in the correct order of departure. The locomotives being moved are 'L1' No 67703, 'F6' No 67220 and 'J15' No 65422. No 65110 entered service in November 1900 as GER No 1160 and rebuilt to the form seen here in May 1928; withdrawal came in March 1955. *Dr Ian C Allen E2837*

Top: The 11.55 from Yarmouth South Town was timetabled to depart Ipswich at 2.15pm with the Liverpool Street service and is seen passing the shed with Class B12/3 No 61535 in charge. The site of the depot was later cleared and is now a housing estate. *Dr Ian C Allen E3302*

Bottom: Just to the south of the locomotive depot a branch led to Griffin Quay which was on the west bank of the River Orwell where Class J15 No 65388 is seen shunting the sidings outside the Waterside Works of Ransomes & Rapier (R&R) who were a major manufacturer of railway equipment and later cranes, from 1869 to 1987. Originally an offshoot of the major engineering company Ransome's, the company was formed in 1869 by four engineers – James Allen Ransome (1806-1875), his elder son, Robert James Ransome (c.1831-1891), Richard Christopher Rapier (1836-1897) and Arthur Alec Bennett (1842-1916) – who left the parent firm by agreement to establish a new firm on a site on the River Orwell to continue the business of manufacturing railway equipment and other heavy works. R. C. Rapier had been head of Ransome's Orwell Works railway department since he joined the business in 1862. When the two businesses were split he became the engineering partner in the new firm known as Ransomes & Rapier at the Waterside Ironworks. During World War 1 R&R produced shells, guns and tank turrets. The Stokes mortar was invented by managing director and chairman Sir Wilfred Stokes, he received a knighthood for the invention. One unexpected use for the R&R 'turn-table' design was for the revolving restaurant in the Post Office (later BT) Tower in London – however this closed to the public in 1971 but forms part of the Grade II listing. *Dr Ian C Allen E2879*

Opposite top: Hadleigh station was the terminus of a short branch line from Bentley junction. The line was built by the Eastern Union & Hadleigh Junction Railway, and acquired by the EUR on 8th June 1847, just prior to the opening on 2nd September 1847. The original intermediate stations were at Capel and Raydon Wood – a temporary station at Bentley Church Crossing opened and closed in December 1853. The terminus had goods sidings on both the southwestern and northeastern sides, the latter serving malt houses and which was also used as a running round loop. There was also a small single road timber clad engine shed that closed at the end of passenger services. The decline in passenger numbers using the branch can be seen in the patronage figures, which were 14,447 in 1923 compared to 5,086 just five years later. The LNER closed the line to passenger traffic on 29th February 1932, although freight services lingered on until 19th April 1965.
A proposal to extend services by building a light railway between Hadleigh and Long Melford was reported in the *Haverhill Echo* on 10th March 1900; however nothing came of the proposal. The route from Hadleigh to Raydon Wood is accessible as the Hadleigh Railway Walk. On 9th June 1956 the Railway Enthusiasts Club organised a brake van special that used Class J15 No 65459 for a trip over the line. The malthouses to the right of the image have been demolished although the original brick-built building has been converted into housing. The restored station building is now surrounded by housing.
Dr Ian C Allen E3174

Opposite bottom: Manningtree station was opened by the EUR in 1846, with traffic increasing it was rebuilt in 1899-1901. This station building still serves in railway usage with over one million passengers a year. Immediately east of the station there is a triangle of junctions, known as the Manningtree South, North and East junctions, and originally each double-track junction was controlled by an individual signal box. In 1926 the LNER installed a new power box at Manningtree South that controlled all three junctions. Today, the north to east curve connecting Ipswich with Harwich Town is a single track, having been reduced from double-track and all three sides of the triangle are electrified. Just east of the station is a combination of a road underpass and a level crossing. The underpass has limited height and the parallel level crossing is needed to permit higher vehicles to cross the railway. Former GNR Class C2 No 1016, built at Doncaster Works in October 1898, was redesignated by the LNER as a Class C12, numbered 4016, in July 1926. It was withdrawn in March 1948 never to carry its BR number. Like the locomotive the GER six-wheel Third never saw BR service.
Dr Ian C Allen E381

This page, top: Marks Tey station was opened in 1843 for services on the GER main line, and the branch line to Sudbury followed in 1849. From that date until 1889 the station was known as Marks Tey Junction. The branch is only accessible to trains travelling from Colchester towards London. The opening of the Colne Valley & Halstead Railway off the Sudbury branch in 1860 and the extension of the branch beyond Sudbury via the Stour Valley Railway in 1865 to Cambridge added importance to Marks Tey as a junction, allowing throughtrains to and from Colchester. These passenger services were gradually cut back and the closure of the Sudbury to Cambridge link in March 1967 saw the end of through running. No 61336 is seen heading a northbound express service; built by NBL in August 1948 it was allocated to Stratford in November the same year. It served on East Anglian metals until November 1960 when it was reallocated to Colwick from where it was withdrawn in September 1963. *Dr Ian C Allen E1803*

This page, bottom: The southern end of the Stour Valley line was at Marks Tey where Class E4 No 62788 is seen awaiting departure with a Colchester to Cambridge service. Built in January 1895 as GER No 496 it remained in traffic until March 1958, being withdrawn from Cambridge depot. Behind the train an LMS-designed Class 2MT 2-6-0 and DMU are awaiting their next duties. *Dr Ian C Allen E3498*

Out of Steam

Above: The end of steam for three Class B1s at Trowse Lower junction early in 1964. Nearest the camera is No 61073; built by the NBL in September 1946 it was withdrawn from New England depot, Peterborough, in September 1963 and recycled by R. A. King & Sons, Norwich, the following February. On the other side of the running line are carriage chassis that have had their bodies removed before being modified for the transportation of cars. *Dr Ian C Allen E2144*

Opposite top: Designed by L. B. Billinton for the London, Brighton & South Coast Railway, 'K' class 2-6-0 No 32337 left Brighton Works in September 1913 and was withdrawn from the adjacent depot in December 1962; it was acquired by Kings for recycling. It is seen in the sidings at Trowse, along with Great Western and Southern Railway locomotives, before transfer to the nearby scrapyard. Twenty of the class were ordered by the LBSCR, however, the Grouping of the railway companies in 1923 resulted in only 17 being completed with the other three cancelled. *Dr Ian C Allen S47*

Opposite bottom: Following withdrawal of traffic from the Wymondham-Forncett line it was used for storing carriage stock before being consigned to scrap merchants. Gresley-designed 'Quad Art' set No 77 (Brake Third No E86332E and Thirds Nos E86333/4/5E) carries a large 'COND' denoting its forthcoming demise. The Quad Art sets consisted of four carriages running on five bogies largely used on intensive suburban services, in this case routes out of King's Cross. *Dr Ian C Allen MISC071*

Steam off the Great Eastern

Top: East of Middleton Towers station on the Dereham-King's Lynn line is a connection to around 520 acres of quarries that are still using rail for transporting the extracted sand. A siding for J. Boam & Sons was approved on 1st March 1904. The original connection was accessed from the west end, requiring a reversal into the quarry sidings – today a conveyor belt loads wagons standing on the line. The company had its own standard and narrow gauge lines, operated by steam and internal combustion locomotives. The standard gauge connection to Middleton Towers sand quarries is seen here with Class J69 No 68498 standing on the BR side. The locomotive to the right is the quarry's Hudswell, Clarke 0-6-0ST *Peter*. Built in 1929 it arrived at Middleton in 1955 and was scrapped on site during 1963. *Dr Ian C Allen E2801*

Bottom: In 1921 work commenced on 40 acres of heath at Nacton, north of the River Orwell to the east of Ipswich – which was without utility services and on a single track road to Nacton and unsuitable for heavy vehicles – on the construction of a metal foundry for Crane Ltd; soon the site had all utility services and included the largest private rail sidings in East Anglia. At the end of June 2008 the works poured its last metal, production of iron fittings ceased and heavy engineering came to an end at what was once the largest private-sector employer in Ipswich. The site was cleared and turned into a shopping centre. The company had several locomotives over the years and one of Peckett & Son's standard 0-4-0ST 'R4' class locomotives, works No 2019 built in 1952, is seen here with three open wagons in tow. After 18 years work there it was purchased by a group of enthusiasts and stored at a farm in Saxmundham, Suffolk. Little restoration work was done and it suffered exposure to the weather until purchased by a Quainton Railway Society member in July 1974. The intention was for it to remain in the lined green Peckett livery, however, it left for a private location in Nottinghamshire in 1982, before moving to the Pallot Steam, Motor & General Museum, Jersey, where it is now named *Kestrel*. *Dr Ian C Allen IND427*

Top: A British Sugar plant was located at Sproughton, Ipswich, being one of the many plants to be built after World War 1. Encouraged by the 1925 Sugar Industry (Subsidy) Act, it was built in 1924-25 by the Anglo-Dutch Sugar Co to make Britain more self sufficient in food after shortages during World War 1. Built on a 100-acre site, the main contracting firm were Hal Williams & Co. Most of the original machinery was second-hand; dismantled from a factory in Holland and shipped to Felixstowe docks. The Anglo-Dutch group was the largest of five organisations that built factories in the 1920s; the company also had factories in Cantley, Ely, Kelham and King's Lynn. The original management was Dutch, but in 1936 the British Sugar Corporation was formed, and this and other factories were absorbed. The Sproughton site closed in 2001. The last steam locomotive to be employed, Peckett & Son's standard 0-6-0ST 'R4' class (works No 2000 of 1942), left for preservation in 1977 on the Nene Valley Railway where it remained until 1984. It has visited many heritage railways since 2000 but is now based at Barrow Hill Roundhouse. *Dr Ian C Allen IND486*

Bottom: *Sirapite* the Garrett works shunter is an unusual and rare shunting engine with an identity problem! Being part traction engine and part locomotive, produced by traction engine manufacturer Aveling & Porter (works No 6158) in 1906 for Gypsum Mines Ltd. It was purchased by Richard Garrett & Sons in 1929 to shunt goods wagons between its works and Leiston station. In 1962 *Sirapite* retired after many years of service, later being bought for preservation by Sir William MacAlpine. In 2003 it was brought by the Long Shop Museum, Leiston, for restoration; after many years and over £50,000 of lottery money it is back in steam at the place it worked at. Located at the heart of the original Richard Garrett & Sons' Town Works, the museum tells an inspiring story of enterprise and endeavour through its stunning collections, hands-on displays and the remarkable family behind the factory. It's actually called 'The Long Shop' as it was the world's first purpose built workshop for assembly line production and as its output grew, it was staffed by engineers who designed and made ploughs, steam engines, peat harvesters, trolley buses, washing machines and more, which were exported across the world. As pioneers in the field of agricultural machinery the Garretts became figureheads and patrons of the local community. *Dr Ian C Allen IND449*

Bibliography and Further Reading

Books
A multitude of books were referred to, and along with various Middleton Press titles. *Railway Bylines* magazine carries useful articles covering light railways, country lines and the smaller motive power used on them. The following proved to be useful sources of information.

Anon, *British Railways Atlas 1947 (2nd Edition) and RCH Junction Diagrams*; Ian Allan Publishing, 2016

Anon, *British Railways Pre-Grouping Atlas and Gazetteer (4th Edition) and RCH Junction Diagrams*; Ian Allan Publishing, 2015

Brodribb, J.; *Branches & Byways: East Anglia*, 9780860935490, OPC, 2000

Brodribb, J.; *The Main Lines of East Anglia*, 9780860936299, OPC, 2009

Butt, R. V. J.; *The Directory of Railway Stations*; PSL, 1995

Cobb, M. H.; *The Railways of Great Britain: A Historical Atlas*, 071103236X; Ian Allan Publishing, 2003

Darsley, R.; *The Wissington Railway: A Fenland Enterprise*; Industrial Railway Society, 0901096490, 1984

Dench, G. & Dench, L.; *Passengers No More* (3rd Edition); Ian Allan, 1980

Digby, N. J. L.; *The Stations and Structures of the Midland & Great Northern Joint Railway: Vol 1 Lowestoft to Melton Constable*, 9781899889822, Lightmoor, 2014

Digby, N. J. L.; *The Stations and Structures of the Midland & Great Northern Joint Railway: Vol 2 Norwich to Peterborough and Little Bytham*, 9781911030816, Lightmoor, 2015

Fell, M. G.; *An Illustrated History of the Port of King's Lynn and its Railways*; 9781906919528, Irwell Press, 2012

Gammell, C. J.; *LNER Branch Lines*, 9780860935094, OPC, 1993

Gordon, D. I.; *A Regional History of the Railways of Great Britain: Volume 5 The Eastern Counties*, 0715374311, David & Charles

Grant, D. J.; *Directory of the Railway Companies of Great Britain*, 9781788037686, Matador, 2017

Griffiths, R. & Smith, P.; *The Directory of British Engine Sheds and Principal Locomotive Servicing Points: Vol 1*, 9780860935426, 1999

Hawkins, C.; *Great Eastern in Town & Country: Vol 1*, 9780871608168, Irwell Press, 1990

Hawkins, C.; *Great Eastern in Town & Country: Vol 2*, 9780871608250, Irwell Press, 1991

Hawkins, C. & Reeve, G.; *Great Eastern Railway Engine Sheds: Vol 1*, 0906867401, Wild Swan, 1986

Hawkins, C. & Reeve, G.; *Great Eastern Railway Engine Sheds: Vol 2*, 0906867487, Wild Swan, 1987

Jenkins, S. C.; *The Cromer Branch*, 0853613842, Oakwood, 1989

Jenkins, S. C.; *The Lynn and Dereham Railway*, 0853614421, Oakwood, 1993

Jenkins, S. C.; *The Lynn and Hunstanton Railway and the West Norfolk Branch*, 08536133303, Oakwood, 1987

Jenkins, S. C.; *The Wells-next-the Sea Branch, via Wymondham and Dereham*, 0853613745, Oakwood, 1988

Jowett, A.; *Jowett's Railway Atlas of Great Britain & Ireland*; PSL, 1989

Kay, P.; *Great Eastern in Town & Country: Vol 3*, 9780871608748, Irwell Press 1996

Longworth, H.; *British Railways Steam Locomotives 1948-1968*, 9780860935933, OPC, 2005

Longworth, H.; *British Railways Steam Locomotive Allocations*, 9780860936428, OPC, 2011

Longworth, H.; *British Railways Pre-Nationalisation Coaching Stock; Vol 1 GWR & LNER*; 9780860936756, OPC, 2018

Paye, P.; *The Mid-Suffolk Light Railway*, 090686741X, Wild Swan, 1986

Paye, P.; *The Waveney Valley Railway: Tivetshall to Beccles*; 9781911038580, Lightmoor Press, 2019.

Online
One of the richest sources of information, with sites covering disused stations; closing dates by year; and individual companies. Perhaps the most interesting is the National Library of Scotland's Ordnance Survey collection.